Puritans, Quakers and Witches

Five Hundred Years of the Haight Family

ISBN 978-1-990543-10-4

All photos from family sources, unless otherwise stated.

Edited by Daphne Ffoulkes-Jones and David Holmes. Copy-edited by Kerry Davie.

Cover and interior design by Kim Lajeunesse.

Interviews and quotes as of June 2023.

Published by NextGen Story: Custom Publishing.

www.nextgenstory.com

In Memory of

Donna Loreen Haight Hadden

January 26, 1936 – May 28, 2022

Table of Contents

The Train vii

Storytellers ix

PART 1 | People

The Hoyt-Haight Family 1
Thomas Hoyte—First Generation 7
Michael Hoyte—Second Generation 9
Simon Hoyte—Third Generation 11
Moses Hoyt I—Fourth Generation 17
Moses Hoyt II—Fifth Generation 20
Moses Hoyt III—Sixth Generation 22
Joseph Haight—Seventh Generation 24
Joseph Haight—Eighth Generation 26
Daniel Haight 28
Quaker Marriages - Adolphustown Community 43
Joel Haight—Ninth Generation 46
Hay Bay Quaker Cemetery 48
Haight Burials—Hay Bay Quaker Cemetery 49
Zachariah Haight—Tenth Generation 51
Quakers, Haights, and the War of 1812 in Upper Canada 54
Thomas Henry Haight—Eleventh Generation 57
The Haights and the Goodmurphys 61
Clarence Adelbert "Del" Haight—Twelfth Generation 63
Walter Stanley Haight—Thirteenth Generation 67
Music in the Genes 69
Walter Stanley Haight—Thirteenth Generation 71
The Haight Women 79
Other Kin 83

PART II | Places

Home Sweet Home ⋯⋯⋯⋯⋯⋯⋯⋯⋯⋯⋯⋯⋯⋯⋯⋯⋯ 93
Island Life in Canada ⋯⋯⋯⋯⋯⋯⋯⋯⋯⋯⋯⋯⋯⋯⋯ 95
Perils of the Waters ⋯⋯⋯⋯⋯⋯⋯⋯⋯⋯⋯⋯⋯⋯⋯⋯ 98
Ferrying through the Years ⋯⋯⋯⋯⋯⋯⋯⋯⋯⋯⋯⋯ 100
The House on Poverty Hill ⋯⋯⋯⋯⋯⋯⋯⋯⋯⋯⋯⋯ 105
The Haights' Story Continues ⋯⋯⋯⋯⋯⋯⋯⋯⋯⋯ 109

APPENDIX A

Family Quilt ⋯⋯⋯⋯⋯⋯⋯⋯⋯⋯⋯⋯⋯⋯⋯⋯⋯⋯⋯⋯ 113
Generations ⋯⋯⋯⋯⋯⋯⋯⋯⋯⋯⋯⋯⋯⋯⋯⋯⋯⋯⋯⋯ 114

APPENDIX B

Family Members Elected or Appointed to Public Office ⋯⋯ 117

The Train

By Jean d'Ormesson

At birth, we boarded the train and met our parents— and we believe that they will always travel by our side. As time goes by, other significant people will board the train of our lives: our siblings, friends, children, strangers, and even the love of our life. However, at some station our parents will step down from the train, leaving us to continue this journey alone. Others will step down over time as well, leaving a permanent vacuum. Some, however, will pass so unnoticed that we won't even realize they have vacated their seats.

This train ride will be full of joy, sorrow, fantasy, expectations, hellos, goodbyes, and final farewells. Success consists of having a good relationship with all the passengers we encounter along the way, which requires us to give the best of ourselves every mile of the journey.

The great mystery for everyone is this: We don't know at which station we will step down. So, we must live in the best way possible by loving, forgiving, and offering the best of who we are. It's important to do this because when the time comes for us to finally step down and leave our empty seat, we should only leave behind beautiful memories for those who will continue to travel on the never-ending train of life.

I wish for you to have a joyful journey on your personal train of life. Reap success, give lots of love, and always remember to be happy. More importantly, thank God for the journey. Lastly, I want to thank you for being one of the passengers on my train.

Storytellers

In each family there seems to be one who is called upon to seek and find their ancestors, to put flesh on the bones, and to make them live again. This individual has been put on earth to tell the family stories, and to feel that somehow, those who have gone before will know and approve. To me, doing genealogy research is not merely the gathering of facts, figures, dates, and anecdotes. It's about breathing life into all who have gone before. We are the storytellers of the tribe; all tribes have one. It's as though we have been called upon to do this, as it were, by our very genes.

In a way, those who have gone before cry out to us to tell their story. So, we do. In finding them, we also somehow find ourselves. How many graves have I stood before? How many elders have I spent time talking with and recording their stories? This goes beyond documenting facts. Their bones are my bones, and their flesh is my flesh. It demonstrates pride in what our ancestors were able to accomplish and pride in how they contributed to both what and who we are today. It goes beyond the resolute determination that they needed to continue and to build a life for their family. It generates a sense of enduring pride for how they fought to make and keep us. It arrives at a deep and immense understanding that they were doing it not merely for themselves, but for us— that we might be born, live, become who we are today, and finally, remember them so that their contribution wouldn't be lost in the darkness of times past. Therefore, we students of the past do this, with love and caring. We painstakingly scribe each fact of their existence— because we are them and they are us.

I am not a Haight by blood, but through the adoption of my father. I was born a Haight, and I treasure having been part of the Haight family. It has been my identity for my entire life. I am so grateful to those who provided stories about this family and their everyday life experiences including the places they lived, the challenges they endured, and the personal memories they shared. These include (but are not limited to): Friends of the Island (Cockburn), Adolphustown Fredericksburgh Heritage Society, St. Joseph Island Historical Society, St. Joseph Island – Our Heritage, Sheila Campbell, Sherry McCaig Beaton, Donna Joan Ouellette and Kathie Baggett for her invaluable advice. I give a huge and special thanks to my aunt, Donna Haight Hadden, for being so patient while answering my many questions. She jokingly commented that had she known there was going to be a test seventy-five years later, she would have paid closer attention. Her personal memories and intimate stories added great depth and feeling to the narrative.

I also obtained information from the research done by professional genealogists, from government documents, and from church, birth, marriage, and death records. All of this information is as accurate as the published documents they came from. That is not to say that as techniques and research improve over the years that none of this information will change in the future. For example, early research from the 1800s stated that the family name originated in Germany, and that Simon Hoyte was from Upwey, about 80 km south of his actual birthplace in Somerset England. It also stated that Simon's first marriage was to Debra Stowers. Later and more detailed research, DNA, and technology have disproven these statements and the corrections are now well documented.

Some of the words and language that have been used in the text, such as Negro and Indian and other such words and phrases, reflect those used during the period, or from a quote used during an earlier time. They are merely part of the record and are not meant to be offensive, insensitive, or derogatory.

As you can imagine, the Hoyt-Haight family have expanded to thousands of descendants over the past five hundred years. This story is based on the direct male descendants over thirteen generations, beginning with Thomas Hoyte (1520–after 1575) and concluding with my grandfather Walter Stanley Haight (1908–1981). We will journey with them from their homes in England to the colonies in America, and their eventual escape to Upper Canada. We will discover how historical events, hardships, triumphs, religion, and the places that they lived shaped them, and in turn made us who we are.

Writing this story has been a great joy for me. My hope is that another storyteller will come along after me—someone who will carry on this work and who will continue to record the interesting and diverse lives of the Haight family for years and decades to come.

Nancy Haight Penrose

PART 1 | People

The Hoyt-Haight Family

There are various spellings of the Haight name: Hoyt, Hoyte, Hait, and Hyatt, all of which are of the same origin. The name Hoyt is derived from the Middle English word hoit, meaning long stick, a word that was used in medieval times as a nickname for tall or skinny men. The surname Haight means someone who lives at the top of a hill.

Although I don't recall meeting too many tall, skinny men in the family, Clarence Adelbert Haight and Walter Stanley Haight both lived in the area known as "The Mountain" on St. Joseph Island (in the north part of Lake Huron), so living at the top of a hill certainly applied in their case. In England, the name appears as Hoyte, then in the United States as Hoyt. After about four generations of this branch in the United States, the surname Haight began to be used consistently.

DNA testing of the Hoyt descendants indicates that they carry a genetic marker that is rather rare in England and Europe, but common in North Africa and places such as Cyprus, Egypt, and Israel. The DNA results suggest that the Simon Hoyt family could well be descended from ancient traders or perhaps merchants of African, Iberian, Carthaginian/ Canaanite or even Jewish or Muslim origin.

Purchased from House of Names (Coat of Arms Store)

In the distant past, migration and trade were common among people from North Africa, Spain, Ireland, and Cornwall. Therefore, ancestors of the Simon Hoyt family could well be Celts with some Iberian or Carthaginian blood. But in the absence of any actual historical records, it is simply a guess as to why (or even how) the Simon Hoyt family inherited genetic markers that point to places like Spain, Italy, North Africa, Cyprus, Egypt, and Israel. The simple fact is— they just do.

The earliest known record of the Hoyte family name in England is associated with Somersetshire. The record is from the reign of King Henry V in the early 1400s. It is discussed in the 1871 Hoyt genealogy:

At the residences of William W. Munckton, Coroner, of Curry Rivel, Somersetshire, the author was allowed to examine various old manuscripts collected by the gentleman... Mr. Munckton has since written that he has found in the court roll of Curry Rivel, 4 and 5 Henry V., 1417 and 1418, the name of John Hoyt, of Curry Rivel, who appears to have been a baker. This is the earliest mention of the name that we have been able to find.[1]

This would tell us that the Hoyts were living in Somerset at least 170 years before our ancestor Thomas.

I first became interested in these ancestors when I discovered the connection of the Puritans and the Quakers (otherwise known as the "Society of Friends") to the Haight family. It's noted that Simon Hoyte (1590–1657) was a Puritan and that he came to what is now America during the Massachusetts Great Migration, somewhere around 1629. Puritans were English Protestants living in the sixteenth and seventeenth centuries, who sought to purify the Church of England of all Roman Catholic practices. They maintained that the Church of England had not been fully reformed and should therefore become more Protestant. They believed in the Five Points of Calvinism (which was founded by John Calvin): (1) Total depravity, (2) That salvation or damnation was predetermined by God, (3) Limited atonement, (4) Irresistible grace, and (5) Perseverance of the Saints.

Puritans were known to be of strong character, which has shown itself in the Hoyt/Haight family for generations. On July 23, 1866, the Hoyt family held a reunion in Panama, New York. The Hoyt family's character was described as follows:

[1] David W. Hoyt, A Genealogical History of the Hoyt, Haight, and Hight Families: With Some Account of the Earlier Hyatt Families, A List of the First Settlers of Salisbury and Amesbury, Mass., Etc (Boston: Providence Press Co., 1871), 275.

Hoyt Family Meeting in Panama, New York. June 1866.
Photograph. Stamford Historical Society, 1999.

Timothy Hoyt's and Abraham van Wie's Hoyt and van Wie History (website), John E Hoyt,
updated March 12, 2023, simonhoyt.com/cayuga-ny.html.

*It is in the tenacity with which we cling to our opinions,
the vigor with which we maintain [them], and the courage
[with] which we proclaim them. We do not take kindly to any
interference from others, with those views of ours that we
consider essential. We will not permit any doubt to arise in
our own minds as to their correctness. We are inclined to be
intolerant and ostracize from our society all those that call
them in question. This characteristic is one of the legacies
inherited by us from our Puritan and Calvinistic ancestors.*[2]

Other Puritan legacies of the Hoyts/Haights are
adventurousness, hard work, skills, and ambition—traits
that seem to have been carried through the genes for more
than five hundred years. Puritans placed a great emphasis
on the importance of work, and the similarities of the work

[2] David Webster Hoyt, Record of the Hoyt Family Meeting: Held at Stamford Connecticut,
June 20 and 21, 1866 (Boston: 1866)

that the Hoyt/Haight men did over the generations are rather interesting. Several of the Hoyt-Haight men, going back hundreds of years and in more recent times worked in road maintenance were landowners, and held public office. They have been and continue to be artisans, musicians, and craftsmen, and they have always seemed to have a penchant for saving animals. This goes back to the early days of the Massachusetts Bay Colony when the Puritans developed and enacted the very first animal protection laws in the Western world in 1641.

My research found a Quaker connection from the 1700s when Moses Haight III married Rachel Dean. At some point they became members of the Society of Friends. It is noted in A Genealogical Narrative of the Daniel Haight Family by his grandson Canniff Haight, that all or nearly all of the family who moved to New York State and to adjoining states were Quakers or became members of the Society immediately afterward.[3]

The founding principles of Quakerism are integrity, equality, simplicity, community, stewardship of the earth, and peace. Quakers played a key role in both the abolitionist and women's rights movements, and in the nineteenth century, many leaders of the women's suffrage movement in the United States were Quakers. In fact, they believed so strongly that all people are equal that they even refused to remove their hats to those in authority or those considered financially or socially their superior. In 1758, Quakers in Philadelphia were ordered to stop buying and selling slaves, and by the 1780s all Quakers were barred from owning them. In the following century, Canadian relatives of the Haight branch, John and Hannah Haight of Pickering, in Upper Canada took in a runaway slave named George Gumby, a sixteen-year-old boy who appears in the 1861 census as a "coloured boy and

---

[3] Canniff Haight, A Genealogical Narrative of the Daniel Haight Family (Legare Street Press, 2022 (originally published 1899)), 16.

student" living with John and Hannah. He may very well have escaped through the Underground Railway and found refuge with the Haight family through the existing Quaker network.

Quakers also have a long history of advocating for animal rights. They became the first denomination to establish an organization focused on stopping animal experimentation. I would be curious to know how many horses, cattle, and in later years, dogs and cats have been rescued from an otherwise deplorable life were it not for a Haight?

Over the last five hundred years, the Hoyte, Hoyt, and Haights have been found in England, the United States, Canada and elsewhere around the world. It is even due to their steadfast religious convictions that two significant migrations occurred. Simon Hoyte, of whom much has already been written, was among a small group of Puritans that was the first to leave England to establish colonies in what is now the United States, particularly in Massachusetts and in Connecticut. This decision helped to bring the Haights to the New World. Daniel Haight, the youngest son of Joseph Haight (1724–1816), was the individual who later moved this branch of the family to Canada. As a Quaker, Daniel practiced pacifism, and so due to his rejection of the American Revolution, the Haights are Canadian by accident of both religion and revolution. This book places an emphasis on the Haights' arrival to Canada, and the generations and locations of significance that were to follow.

As you encounter the story of the Haight family in Part I, you will discover strong characters with unshakable convictions and adventurous spirits—and a few surprises along the way, like the witches from the title of this book.

Thomas Hoyte—First Generation

Eleven Silver Spoons

Thomas Hoyte was born around 1520 in Seavington St. Mary, Somersetshire, England. Two copies of the will of Thomas Hoyte of "Sevington Marye" (now Seavington St. Mary), county of Somerset, dated November 10, 1576, are currently found at Wells, England. In it, he mentions his wife, Isabell; his sons, John, Roberte, Thomas the elder, Thomas the younger, Roger, Michael, and Richard; and his daughters, Mary and Christian, both of whom were at the time unmarried. He also mentions his grandchildren, Joane or Johan, daughter of his son John; John, son of his son Thomas the elder; William, son of his son Thomas the younger; and Roger, son of his son Roger.

He gifted land to his son Roger, and, besides disposing of sheep, cows, etc., gave silver spoons to each one of his sons, and wished that after the death of his sons that the spoons be passed down to their children. He also made a bequest to the poor and the church of that parish. This gives us an idea of Thomas's social and financial status. Thomas Hoyte the elder was one of the two witnesses to his father's will. In the probate record his name is spelled Hoite, and his wife, Isabelle Hoite, is appointed executrix. Research has been unable to determine his exact date of death, but we must assume that it was sometime after 1575, since his will was dated 1576.

Church of St. Mary, Seavington where Thomas Hoyte bequeathed money to the poor.

Michael Hoyte—Second Generation

Stray Sheep and Public Office

Michael Hoyte was born in about 1560 in West Hatch, Somerset, England. He is the sixth son of Thomas Hoyte and wife Isabell. His name first appears in a July 18, 1599, Manor Court record that pertains to his occupation of rented land, apparently in West Hatch, Somersetshire. This document refers to the customary rent, services and works of scouring and ditching the lord's rivers in exchange for the tenancy of Michael Hoyte and his family. It is interesting to note that in Britain at this time, all land was ultimately owned by the Crown. If you performed services for the Crown, you were provided land in exchange. In some cases, depending upon the agreement with the Crown, the occupier could rent out or sublet portions of the property, for example, to their children.

Michael later occupied other properties and served in various positions in the town offices. From 1606 to 1620 he was a juryman and often served as foreman of the homage jury in the Halimote Court and Manor Court.

In 1612–1613 Michael was a reeve, or a "keeper of animals," on behalf of the town. Any horses or other livestock found running at large within the town limits were impounded. The owner would be subject to a penalty of ten shillings for each animal, as well as poundage fees. If these fees were not paid within twenty-four hours, Michael as reeve would post notice in three of the most public places in the town, providing a description of the livestock and specifying the time when the animals would be sold. All funds collected by Michael were delivered to the treasurer of the town. In 1613 he had five stray sheep in his custody.

Michael was elected a "tythingman" or tax collector at West Hatch in 1614. That same year he also served as a reeve, with records indicating that he was holding a horse that was to be given to the lords as a fee for someone's tenancy. Michael was a respected and trusted member of the town to be assigned these responsible and important positions, but he probably was not very well liked by those he had to collect fees and taxes from. In Halimote Court records, Michael stated that in 1617 he surrendered his 1599 rental lands to the use of his son Simon.

Simon Hoyte—Third Generation

Voyage to Massachusetts Bay Colony

Simon Hoyte, son of Michael Hoyte, was an adventurous man. He was born sometime around 1590 in West Hatch, Somersetshire, England, and is the eighth great grandfather of Walter Stanley Haight. Simon was among a small group who sailed to the New World with the intention of starting a new life in Charlestown, in the Massachusetts Bay Colony. Like Simon, most of these individuals were of high social status or gentry and they were convinced that their Puritan beliefs would enable them to establish a Eutopia of like-minded individuals in this new setting. They sailed aboard the ship the Lyon's Whelp in 1629.

The Lyon's Whelp was part of the Higginson Fleet and it left the River Thames, Gravesend, England on April 25, 1629 along with five other ships: George Bonaventure, Four Sisters, Lyon, Mayflower (not the famous Mayflower of the Pilgrims) and Talbot. Their destination was Massachusetts Bay, the purpose was to establish a colony, and the voyage became known as the Massachusetts Great Migration.

The catalyst for this journey was the Puritans'—of which Simon was one—desire for religious independence from the Church of England. Puritans left England primarily due to religious persecution but also for economic reasons. The Thirty Years' War (1618–1648), which pitted Protestants against Catholics, had a huge impact on the overall economy of Europe. Wars cost money, and the more affluent citizens wanted to distance themselves from both the financial repercussions and the hostility and threats levied against religious non-conformists such as the Puritans.

There were two different types of Puritans at the time: separatists and non-separatists. The non-separatists wanted to remain within the church and to reform it from the inside.

Lyon's Whelp.

The separatist Puritans felt the church was too corrupt to reform and instead wanted to separate from it entirely. This action presented a problem because, in England, the church and state were considered as one, and the very act of separating from the Church of England was considered treasonous. Simon Hoyte and the other Puritans of the Massachusetts Bay Colony were non-separatists and they wanted to remain part of the Church of England, with the ability to select their own ministers and to decide on their own rules.

The Puritans were seeking freedom, but they didn't seem to understand the concept of tolerance. They went to America to find religious freedom—but only for themselves.

Before the voyage began, much preparation was needed. Each man was required to bring provisions for the journey, as well as everything that he would need to establish a plantation.

There were three classes of passengers: those who paid for their passage, those who had a profession such as an art or a trade and were to receive money or grants of land, and those who paid a part of their passage and were to work at the rate of three shillings a day after their arrival to pay for their transport. Indentured servants (essentially slaves) traveled at the expense of their master, who received fifteen acres of land for each servant transported. Passengers were also responsible for paying the cost of shipping household goods. An average eight-member family transporting one ton of freight would foot a bill for thirty pounds sterling. Since Simon was a man of means, he would have paid the passage and freight costs for himself and his family. In today's money the cost would be about US$9,000.

Onboard the ships were three hundred-fifty men, women, and children, one hundred-fifteen head of cattle (which included) cows, horses, oxen, forty-one goats, and some rabbits. These vessels were simply not designed to transport passengers for a two-to-three-month journey. Temporary makeshift cabins located between decks were installed to provide protection from the elements. There were no bathrooms, heat, or light. Women and children spent a good part of the voyage below deck. In keeping with their faith, each day opened and closed with the reading of a chapter in the Bible, singing, and of course with prayers.

On May 27 there was a tremendous storm and rain fell on the fleet in torrents. Waves poured over the ships, filling them with water. Some passengers were afflicted with smallpox, with one five-year-old child dying and having to be buried at sea. Others became sick with scurvy due to the problems of providing fresh food during a long sea voyage. The livestock didn't fare much better, as seventy died during the voyage. In mid-June, one man and a second child also died.

Land was finally sighted on June 24. On June 27 Simon and his shipmates anchored at an old fishing station. Some men went ashore and returned with freshly picked strawberries and gooseberries—which must have been received by the passengers as true gifts from heaven. On June 30 they finally arrived at their destination. They planted their feet on dry land after spending eight weeks at sea and traversing more than three thousand miles of open water. This had not been a journey for the faint of heart. Leaving England, family, and everything they had known behind, and heading into an unknown world must have been a daunting experience for Simon and his family.

In 1630 we find Simon living in Dorchester, Massachusetts with his name appearing in the Town of Dorchester records as Simon Hoit. He remained in Dorchester until 1635 when it was ordered:

that the lott of meadow that was Simon Hoyte's, next to Boston side joyning to John Witchfield, shall be divided betwixt, Mr. Roger Williams and Gyles Gibbs.[4]

On May 18, 1631, Simon was made a freeman—one of the first in Massachusetts. This designation had nothing to do with

---

[4] "New York Beginnings: Information About Simon Hoyt," Genealogy.com, Elizabeth Stuerke, accessed March 1, 2022, genealogy.com/ftm/s/t/u/Elizabeth-Stuerke-IL/WEBSITE-0001/UHP-0250.html.

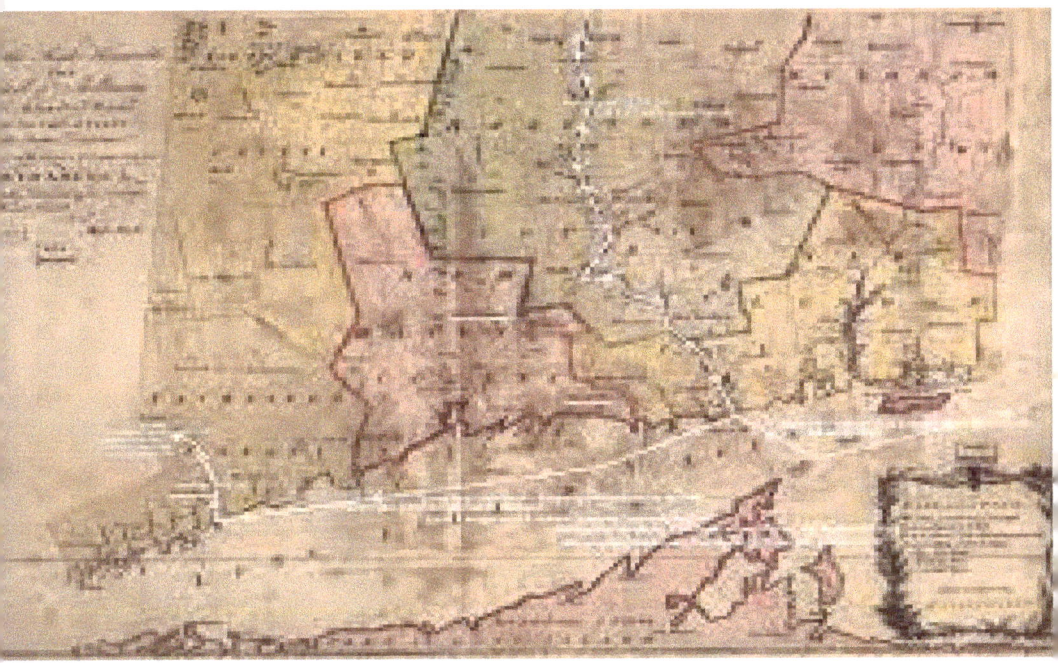

Simon Hoyt's Migration from the Massachusetts Bay Colony.

"Simon Hoyt Family Migration," Simon Hoyte (website), John E Hoyt, updated January 4, 2020, www.simonhoyt.com/ridgefield-ct.html.

slavery or former slavery, but referred to a person's position in his church and community. The position of freeman had to be earned by those who settled among the New England Puritans. He and his second wife joined the church at Scituate, Massachusetts on April 19, 1635.

It's believed that Simon was married twice. West Hatch parish church records indicate that he first married Jane Stoodlie. Together they had five children, Walter, Nicholas, Alexander, John, and Agnes. Another son, Christopher (1616–1617), may have been born before Simon married Jane.

Simon later married Susannah (surname unknown), with whom he had seven children. In 1639, the family moved southwest to Windsor, Connecticut.

Simon was obviously a restless spirit. He helped establish several towns in the wilderness, and in doing so accumulated property along the way. He personified the "pioneer spirit"

Monument in Windsor, Connecticut dedicated to the first settlers, which includes Simon Hoyt.

"Founders of Windsor," HMdb.org (The Historical Marker Database) (website), by Michael Herrick, revised November 5, 2021, hmdb.org/m.asp?m=99589.

and left his mark on his country in ways that few other colonists could. In the space of thirty years, Simon lived in seven villages—and he founded at least three of them. His wife must have been a very strong and easy-going individual to have tolerated her home being uprooted about every five years, in order to move on to yet another wilderness area and to start to build all over again.

Simon was never one to stay in one place for too long, and we eventually find him in Stamford, Fairfield, Connecticut, his last home and final resting place. He died there on September 1, 1657. It is suggested in the book Story of Early Settlers of Stamford, Connecticut, 1641–1700, Including Genealogies of Principal Families by Jean Majdalany that, at the time of Simon's death, a malaria epidemic was devastating the community, and that Simon may well have fallen victim.

Moses Hoyt I—Fourth Generation

The Oath of a Freeman

Moses Hoyt/Haight received recognition and commendations throughout his life. He was the second oldest child of Simon Hoyt and his second wife Susannah, and he was born in about 1634 in Dorchester, Massachusetts.

In 1658 he married Elizabeth Budd and on November 1, 1659, he became a freeman. This was significant as it gave him much greater standing in both the church and the community. In the colonies, the church and the secular authority went hand in hand, and they exercised great power over every aspect of an individual's life. There were harsh punishments for those who deviated from the rules.

The Puritans, as Congregationalists, believed that each congregation would be self-governing. Their way of governing was authoritarian, from the top on down. They were not interested in individual freedoms, democracy, religious toleration, or separation of church and state. For a man (no women were allowed) to participate in the hierarchy of this group, he had to take the freeman's oath. This allowed him to vote, govern, and to have full status in the church and the community. This was essentially a loyalty oath.

Although he was born in the colony, Moses would be required to meet the same requirements as someone born outside the colony in order to become a freeman. Moses would be considered a settler and not considered free. His actions and activities were closely monitored by the hierarchy to ensure that they fit with the church's ideal. If Moses proved himself fit with this ideal, in other words if he joined the church, paid his debts, was owing to no man, and was under no judicial restraints, then he would be accepted by the hierarchy and would be allowed to take the freeman's oath. This process of acceptance took some time because he had to prove himself worthy and had to become a member in good standing of the congregation.

In this oath, Moses would have had to swear to uphold the governing body, not conspire against the commonwealth, and not take any action that would threaten or overthrow the existing government. Only freemen could vote to nominate magistrates, deputies, and other representatives, and only freemen could govern.

The freeman's oath was originally written by John Winthrop, the governor of the Massachusetts Bay Colony in 1631. Until 1639, each oath was handwritten in the language of the day, a slightly more modern version of Old English. It was printed for the first time in 1639.

Six years later, in 1665, Moses, along with nine other men and their families, moved from Fairfield, Connecticut to Eastchester, Westchester, New York.

Several historical records indicate that in 1670–1671, Moses received grants of land and served on committees to design the land's lay-out, to mark on a map the highway connecting to it, and to attend to its fences.

On June 26, 1671, because of his status and position, Moses was chosen to deliver a message to the governor of New York. That same year he was ordered to appear in court to answer for a misdeed. Moses acknowledged his wrongdoing, and the court accepted this acknowledgment.

In A Genealogical Narrative of the Daniel Haight Family by Canniff Haight, it notes that in 1682, Moses had the highest tax rate of any freeholder (property owner) in Eastchester.[5] A

---

[5] "New York Beginnings: Information About Simon Hoyt," Genealogy.com, Elizabeth Stuerke, accessed March 1, 2022, genealogy.com/ftm/s/t/u/Elizabeth-Stuerke-IL/WEBSITE-0001/UHP-0250.html.

general tax law was established in 1634 where each man was assessed according to his estate and all other abilities. Since Moses owned several properties and was deemed to have many valuable abilities, his taxes were more than anyone else's in Eastchester. In 1685 Moses was appointed deputy constable. He was also appointed to serve on a committee that would negotiate with Native Indians about land. In 1686, Moses was chosen town commissioner. It's obvious that Moses was a highly regarded and respected individual since he was appointed to and held these important positions in his community.

The pay for a Puritan minister was meager to say the least. It was expected that the wealthier members of the congregation would contribute to their salary. Moses contributed one pound annually toward supporting a minister in Eastchester. As well, Moses was a pew holder in the Eastchester meetinghouse. This again indicated that Moses was a man of some means. To be a pew holder was a sign of both wealth and status.

Moses died in 1712 at the age of seventy-eight in Eastchester, New York. From what we know of him, it seems that he was one of the wealthiest of the Hoyts.

Moses Hoyt II—Fifth Generation

Slave Ownership

The next Hoyt/Haight received wealth, a name—and a slightly more problematic "gift."

Moses Hoyt/Haight II was born around 1662 in Fairfield, Connecticut. He married Elizabeth Shute in 1691 and together they had nine children. (As adults, Moses II's sons used the surname Haight.) Moses's career included serving as a constable in 1693 and as a fence viewer in 1698. The responsibilities of fence viewer would be equivalent to those carried out by our by-law officers today. Appointed by the town, the fence viewer administered fence laws by inspecting new fences and by settling disputes arising from any livestock that had escaped their enclosure.

In 1702, his father, Moses I, deeded Moses II "one half of his home lot in Eastchester, with house and barn thereon, also one negro called Ben."

It is difficult to imagine that members of the Haight family would be slave owners.

At the time, slaves were considered property that could be bought and sold or bequeathed in their owner's will. Most of eighteenth-century society condoned slavery as a normal condition and an economic necessity.

From his will, we know that Moses I had at least one slave, Ben. However, his son Moses II died before his father and there is no record of what eventually happened to Ben. We might assume that he went to another family member or was sold.

We know that other members of the Hoyt/Haight family also owned slaves. Samuel Haight, the grandson of Simon Hoyt, stated in his will in 1711 that his Negro man, Luke, was to be sold. Titus was to be left to his daughter Sarah, Mingo to his daughter Hannah, and Bristo to his daughter Phebe.

Moses was a prosperous man and he contributed much to his community. He acquired several properties throughout his life and upon his death bequeathed each son with several lots. The three younger sons were still minors when Moses died, and they inherited these properties once they reached the age of twenty-one.

Moses II passed away in 1711 at the age of forty-nine, just a short time before his father died.

Moses Hoyt III—Sixth Generation

Joining the Society of Friends (Quakers)

Although the Hoyts/Haights came to North America as Puritans, their views and beliefs changed over time. At some point after 1718, Moses III and his family joined the Society of Friends (Quakers), and this would continue for several generations.

Moses Haight III was born on October 28, 1696, in Eastchester, Westchester, New York. In 1718, Moses married Rachel Dean at Grace Church (Episcopal) in Jamaica, Long Island, New York. They had eight children: six boys and two girls.

Puritans and the Society of Friends both believed that the Church of England was too similar to the Roman Catholic Church and that it should eliminate ceremonies and practices not rooted in the Bible.

The Religious Society of Friends, also referred to as the Quaker Movement, was founded in seventeenth century England by George Fox. He and other early Quakers, or Friends, were persecuted for their beliefs, which included their belief that the presence of God exists in every person. Quakers rejected elaborate religious ceremonies, didn't have official clergy, and believed in spiritual equality for both men and women. Quaker missionaries first arrived in America during the mid-1650s.

There are two distinct categories of Quaker worship services. Some worship services were led by pastors, while others had no pastoral direction. These congregation members practiced in silence, although speaking was permitted if it was inspired. These gatherings were referred to as meetings, while Quakers that had programmed worship used either meeting or church to refer to their congregations. Many, but not all Quakers regard themselves as Christians. Quaker records indicate that Moses III and three of his sons, Moses IV, Joseph, and Solomon, were active members of both the Oblong Friend's and Nine Partners Friend's Meetings.

A primary Quaker belief is that all human beings are equal and worthy of respect. Quakers were among the first white people to denounce slavery in the American colonies and in Europe, while the Society of Friends became the first organization to take a collective stand against both slavery and the slave trade as a whole. Due to this Quaker belief, it is likely that Moses III did not continue to own slaves as his father and grandfather had done.

Moses and his family appear to have moved to the Crum Elbow precinct in Dutchess County, New York in 1741. He died about 1751 at age fifty-five in Stanford, Dutchess, New York.

Joseph Haight—Seventh Generation

A Long Life

Joseph Haight was born about 1724 in Nine Partners, Dutchess, New York and in 1746 he married Mary Ann Palmer in Westchester, New York. They had six sons and one daughter. Their youngest son, Daniel was only four years old when his mother passed away in 1768. After his wife's death, he married his second wife-a woman named Margaret (surname unknown). In 1814, when he was already ninety years old, Joseph wrote his last will and testament. Among the beneficiaries were the children of his sons, Amos and Obadiah, who predeceased him. Those grandchildren received what would have been their parents share. Joseph left to his only daughter Rachel, a bed and bedstead as well as four sheets, four blankets, two pillows, four pillowcases, and two coverlets. Since she was his only daughter, these items would have been more useful to her as it was not common for women to inherit real property or valuable assets at this point in history.

To his son Reuben he left his clock, and to his oldest son Joseph he left his desk. The remainder of his estate was divided equally between his children. Owning a clock during the eighteenth century was almost unimaginable. Each clock was handmade and extremely expensive. Perhaps Reuben had a sentimental attachment to the clock and that is why Joseph left it to him. Joseph was the eldest and that may have been the reason he received his father's desk. During that time period, desks were usually large, ornate, and carved with embellishments. They were usually made for a country house library and were considered a luxury.

Joseph died in 1816 in Washington, Dutchess, New York at the ripe old age of ninety-two, two years after writing his will. Since the average life expectancy of a man during this period was about thirty-eight years, Joseph lived almost two and a half times longer than average. He lived the longest of all the male descendants of Thomas Hoyt. Could his disciplined and pious Quaker lifestyle contributed to that longevity?

Joseph Haight—Eighth Generation

Hiding Tories

Some Quakers followed a specific naming pattern for their children; hence you will often find the eldest son named after their father which is the case here. Unlike Catholics, Quakers tended to stay away from the names of saints such as Mary and Anne. They did tend to use virtue names like Patience, Charity, and Mercy. Boys were often named after someone in the Old Testament, and the Haights were no exception to this practice with names like Obadiah, Amos, and Moses. Two of the more interesting names included Daniel Haight's son Consider Merritt, and Joel Haight's wife Bathsheba.

Joseph Haight was born about 1746 in Nine Partners, Dutchess, New York and was the eldest son of Mary Anne Palmer and Joseph Haight. He was the brother of Daniel Haight. He married Margaret Rogers in 1770. He was a member of the Society of Friends but because he married out of the Nine Partners Society of Friends, he was dismissed on June 6, 1770. Research has been unable to determine whether he was ever reinstated. Unlike with other religions, dismissal was not shunning or excommunication. It only meant that the individual could no longer vote at the Quaker meetings.

A Branch of the Haight Family, a book written in 1944, states that:

During the American Revolution Joseph conducted Tories to the British lines and used his father's farm as a hiding place for these men until it was safe to go on. [6]

---

[6] "The Nebraska and Midwest Genealogical Record, Vol. XXII, Lincoln Nebraska, April 1944, No. 2, page 16;" NEGcnWeb Project Resource Center OLLibrary, Journals (Website); Edited by Raymond E. Dale, by Ted & Carole Miller; accessed fall 2022; http://www.usgennet.org/usa/ne/topic/resources/OLLibrary/Journals/NMGR/Vol22/nmgrp003.html#ba

This would have been a huge risk for both Joseph and his father. Even though their religious beliefs meant that they did not participate in the war, most Quakers supported the British. For the many individuals who were believed to be supporters, there was a climate of fear, and a threat of violence. Rebels could very easily have beaten Joseph and his family, burned their farm, and stolen their assets. They held firm to their convictions and took the risk.

Joseph died in 1817 at the age of sixty-nine in Nine Partners, Dutchess, New York.

At this time wives did not automatically inherit their husbands' assets. Land and farms were generally left to their sons. In his last will and testament, Joseph leaves his wife Margaret and daughter Phebe *"the privilege of the two east rooms of the house in which they now live and also the privilege of space in the cellar of the house."* [7]

Because he had left his house to one of his sons, this was to ensure that his wife and daughter had a home to live in after his death. He also left them three good cows for their use. Joseph's son Amos had predeceased him. In his will he requested that Amos's son be supported and provided schooling until the age of fourteen, and at age twenty-three when he would more than likely be independent and possibly planning to marry, be provided with one bed and chest, one gun, and fifty pounds. Once his daughter, Phebe, married, she would relinquish all privileges provided in the will.

---

[7] Will of Joseph Haight. Register of Wills, Liber E, P. 139, Office Of Clerk of Surrogate Court, Dutchess County, Poughkeepsee, N. Y.

Daniel Haight

The American Revolution and Coming to Canada

Although not a direct male ancestor of mine, Daniel Haight was the youngest son of the elder Joseph Haight (1724–1816). He was the first to leave the United States of America, and he brought with him other Haights—this effectively founded the Canadian branch of the Haight family.

Daniel was born on January 14, 1764, in Dutchess, New York and he was a member of the Society of Friends. By this time, Friends lived throughout the thirteen British colonies in North America, with large numbers located in the Pennsylvania colony in particular.

The American Revolution (1765–1791) and the American Revolutionary War (1775–1783) created a difficult situation for Daniel and many of these Friends (informally known as Quakers) because their nonviolent religious tenets often conflicted with the emerging political and nationalistic ideals of their homeland. Quakers have always been pacifists, and they usually refuse to bear arms during conflict.

Early in the American Revolution, Quakers participated in the revolutionary movement through nonviolent actions such as embargoes and other economic protests. However, the outbreak of war created an ideological divide within the group as most Quakers remained true to their pacifist beliefs and thus refused to support any military actions.

Nevertheless, a sizable number of Quakers still participated in the conflict in some form and had to deal with the repercussions from their Quaker community for doing so. It is said that thirty thousand members of the Society of Friends remained neutral, 1,276 were disowned by the Friends for supporting the Revolution, 239 were disowned for paying taxes in lieu of military service, thirty-two were

John Dorland (1749–1833), father-in-law of Daniel Haight.

disowned for serving on committees for defense, and forty-two were disowned for deviations which included watching military drills and celebrating independence.

Being disowned was harsh treatment for those who were trying to remain neutral but who had then been ordered to participate despite their beliefs. They were in a difficult spot, and often found their farms raided, their horses and cattle stolen by patriot soldiers, and themselves disowned by their religious community if they participated—even if that participation in the war effort had taken place against their will.

Daniel was a Friend, and because of his beliefs he opposed war and bloodshed and he did not bear arms during the Revolutionary War. During this time, the Friends and Loyalists of the Crown suffered severely at the hands of patriot soldiers for their beliefs. They were imprisoned and compelled to contribute to the war effort. In some cases, their property was confiscated and they were expelled from the country.

Boys as young as sixteen were compelled to serve in the militia. There were younger boys that wished to serve, and they were used as messengers or they carried out other menial tasks.

Daniel did not have sympathy for the party that brought about the Revolution. Though he was a Friend, he was a Loyalist at heart and preferred to live under British rule. Loyalists who supported Britain usually had close business ties to Britain, but most often, as they were conservative by nature, they valued order and were sentimental to their homeland. Due to this, in about 1796, Daniel; his son Philip from his first marriage; his second wife, Mary; their four children; Mary's father, John Dorland; and Daniel's nephew, Joel Haight, all left Dutchess County, New York for Upper Canada which was still under British rule. Their long and difficult journey

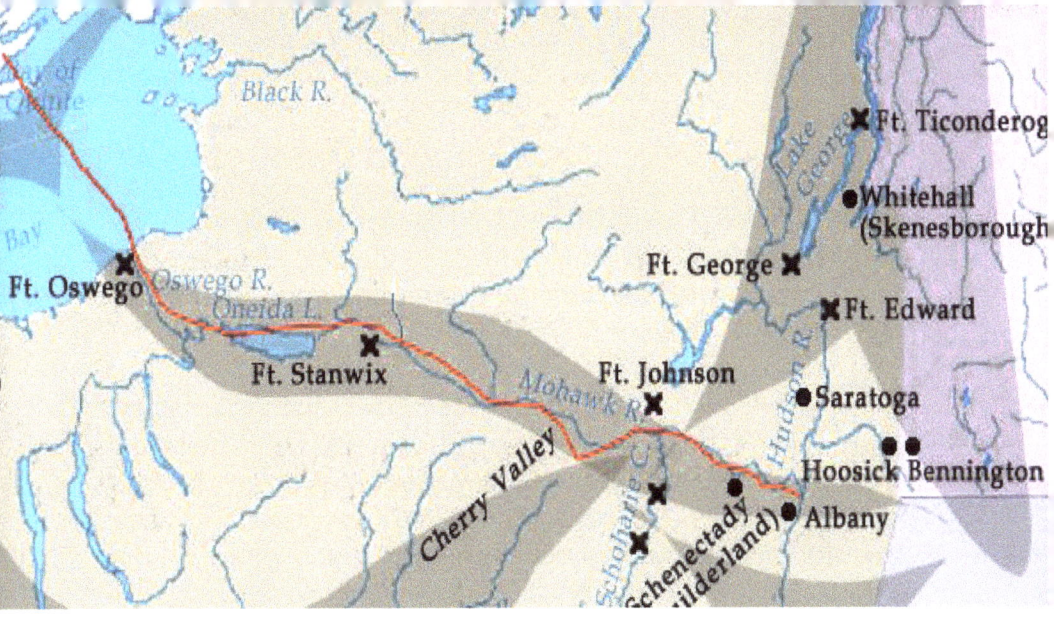

"The route taken from Poughkeepsie to Upper Canada" by Nancy Penrose, Google Maps, Google, updated fall 2022, https://www.google.com/maps.

took them to their destination, Fourth Town, now known as Adolphustown, on the Bay of Quinte in Upper Canada.

The trip started with the group boarding a riverboat on the Hudson River at Poughkeepsie. They travelled north to Troy, New York at the mouth of the Mohawk River near Albany, the state capital. There, they boarded a smaller, shallow draft boat and moved upriver along the Mohawk, west to Rome, New York. Once there, they, and other settlers bound for Upper Canada, loaded their possessions into farm wagons for the overland trek northwest to Lake Oneida where they boarded another boat headed for the Oneida River. After arriving at this river, they took it to where it meets the Oswego River at Three River Point. The journey now took them down the Oswego to Lake Ontario. At this point they chartered a lake sailboat to travel the one hundred kilometers across Lake Ontario to Adolphustown.

The map and geography of upper New York State and what is now Ontario looked very different then than it does today. During the eighteenth century, the river system of New York

State allowed flat-bottomed riverboats to navigate from Poughkeepsie on the Hudson River to the port of Oswego on Lake Ontario with only one long overland crossing of about forty-five kilometers.

It must have been an incredible journey with many hardships. Since much of the route was along forest trails, Indian guides were required. The route also included passage through territory of the Oneida tribe who were allies of the Americans. Hostile American militia detachments actively patrolled the area. Crossing the unpredictable Lake Ontario added to the dangers. However, since this family group was able to bring some of their belongings with them and had the means to hire guides and boats, their circumstances were not quite as desperate as those other refugees who had landed destitute before them.

Preceding them in arriving at Adolphustown were John Dorland's brothers, Thomas and Philip. This area had only been acquired by the British a few years before the brothers' arrival. It had been purchased from the Mississauga First Nation in 1783 before the signing of the Treaty of Paris.

When the United Empire Loyalists first arrived in Upper Canada, many brought their slaves with them. John Dorland's brother, Captain Thomas Dorland, is said to have brought about twenty slaves to Adolphustown in 1784. In 1793, Upper Canada passed the Act to Limit Slavery in Upper Canada to prevent the further introduction of slaves and to limit the term of contracts for servitude. It was not an outright abolishment as compromises were made to satisfy the interests of fifteen members of the legislature who owned slaves, one of the members being Captain Thomas Dorland. After the proclamation of the Act, slaves already in Upper Canada would remain the property of their owners for life. Children born to slaves were to be freed at age twenty-five, children of children born to slaves were free at birth. No slaves could enter the province and any slaves brought into

Upper Canada would be freed automatically and the owners of freed slaves were to provide for their security. It was not until 1833 that Britain abolished slavery throughout the Empire. This law took effect on August 1, 1834, and it freed the last remaining slaves in Upper Canada.

For the first three years of settlement in Upper Canada, the settlers' basic needs were looked after by the government who supplied them with food rations and clothing as well as spring wheat, peas, corn, and potatoes for seed. At the end of that period, the settlers were to provide for themselves. In 1787 crops failed and the Crown rations were ending. Leeks, buds of trees, and leaves were ground up to eat. This was referred to as The Hungry Year due to the shortage of food. The winter had been so harsh even venison and other wild game were difficult to find. If they had bran from the previous year it was boiled in water and for many it was the only meal, they had. If they were able to get potatoes, they planted only the eye and used the rest as food. By 1789, venison, partridge, and pigeons were once again abundant and there were plenty of fish and berries.

Canniff Haight, Daniel's grandson, gives some specifics in his book Country Life in Canada, which was published in 1885.

The Loyalist community suffered terribly against both starvation and the winter cold: at least five people are said to have died in Adolphustown. 'Men were glad, in some cases, to give all they possessed for that which would sustain life. Farms were given in exchange for small quantities of flour, but more frequently refused. A respectable old lady was wont in those days to go away to the woods early in the morning to gather and eat the buds of the basswood, and then bring an apron full home to her family. In one neighbourhood a beef bone passed from house to house and was boiled again and again in order

[8] "Loyalists in Upper Canada," Our Ancestors and Their Times, WordPress, accessed fall 2022, https://ourancestorsandtheirtimes.wordpress.com/loyalists-in-upper-canada-1784-to-1818/

Daniel Haight's Land Grant Request 1797.

"Results: Land Petitions of Upper Canada, 1763-1865," Library and Archives Canada, Government of Canada, accessed fall 2022, https://www.bac-lac.gc.ca/eng/discover/land/land-petitions-upper-canada-1763-1865/Pages/List.aspx?

to extract some nutrient from it.' [8]

In 1797, the year after they arrived in Adolphustown, Joel and Daniel submitted a petition for land.

The Crown land granting process involved dealing with government departments, which even before Confederation was just as complicated as it is today. Due to the American Revolution, many people from the American colonies wanted to settle in British territory. Under the Constitutional Act of 1791, the lands of Upper Canada were to be distributed under the control of, and according to, regulations that the Crown and its representatives made.

By 1795, there was a complex system of land titles and ownership under the direction of the surveyor general. Applicants for a Crown land grant would submit a petition, or application, to the Crown. If the petition was successful, the Crown would approve a land grant, with the petitioner then becoming a settler.

The Executive Council Office, the Receiver General's Office, the Attorney General's Office, the Surveyor General's Office, and the Provincial Secretary's Office were all involved, with each having its own numbering system for the grant documents that it created or received.

If the settler took up residence on the land and fulfilled specific settlement obligations, he would eventually own the land. The settlement duties could include the clearing of the land, the construction of buildings on the land, and the payment of settlement fees. Once the settler fulfilled the settlement duties, the Crown would issue a patent which transferred the land to the settler.

Joel Haight's petition in July 1797 included a letter from Major Peter Van Alstine, Justice of the Peace. Joel received a patent reading,

UPPER CANADA.

COUNCIL-CHAMBER,

NAVY HALL, FEBRUARY 2, 1793.

PRESENT

His Excellency J O H N G R A V E S S I M C O E, Efquire;
Lieutenant-Governor, &c. &c. &c.=IN COUNCIL.

HIS Excellency acquainted the Board, that He wifhed to call their attention to the Situation of the feveral Perfons occupying Lands or claiming to be entitled thereto under various Authorities fince the firft Settlement of the Province, and to confult on the moft effectual means of carrying his Majefty's gracious Intentions into Execution by making out regular grants of Allotments of Land to fuch Perfons as are refpectively entitled thereto.

RESOLVED,

That immediate fteps be taken to fulfill his Majefty's Gracious Intentions progreffively throughout the Province, and that the fame be publicly made known; and for that purpofe that notice be given to all Perfons claiming any Allotment of Land within the HOME DISTRICT of this Province that they do forthwith bring in to the Attorney-General of this Province the certificate, ticket of occupation, warrant, or other document whereon they feverally found their claim; or tranfmit to him an attefted copy thereof, that He may report thereon to his Excellency in Council, in order that regular and effective grants of Eftates of inheritance in the faid allotments may without delay be made out to all perfons entitled thereto conformably to his Majefty's Royal Proclamation, to the Rules and Regulations for the conduct of the Land Office Department heretofore feverally declared and made public, and in purfuance of an Act of Parliament, paffed in the Thirty-firft Year of his prefent Majefty's Reign, entitled, an Act to repeal certain parts of an Act paffed in the Fourteenth Year of his Majefty's Reign, entitled an Act for making more effectual provifion for the Government of the Province of Quebec in North-America, and to make further provifion for the Government of the faid Province.

And further, that due notice fhall from time to time be given to all perfons claiming Lands within the remaining Diftricts of this Province as foon as it fhall be convenient and practicable to proceed on their Claims.

Extracted from the Minutes,

E. B. LITTLEHALES,

Acting Clerk of the Council.

Proclamation by His Excellency, the Lieutenant Governor and Commander in Chief of the Province of Upper Canada on behalf of His Majesty to grant lands of the Crown, February 7, 1792. Toronto Public Library Archives

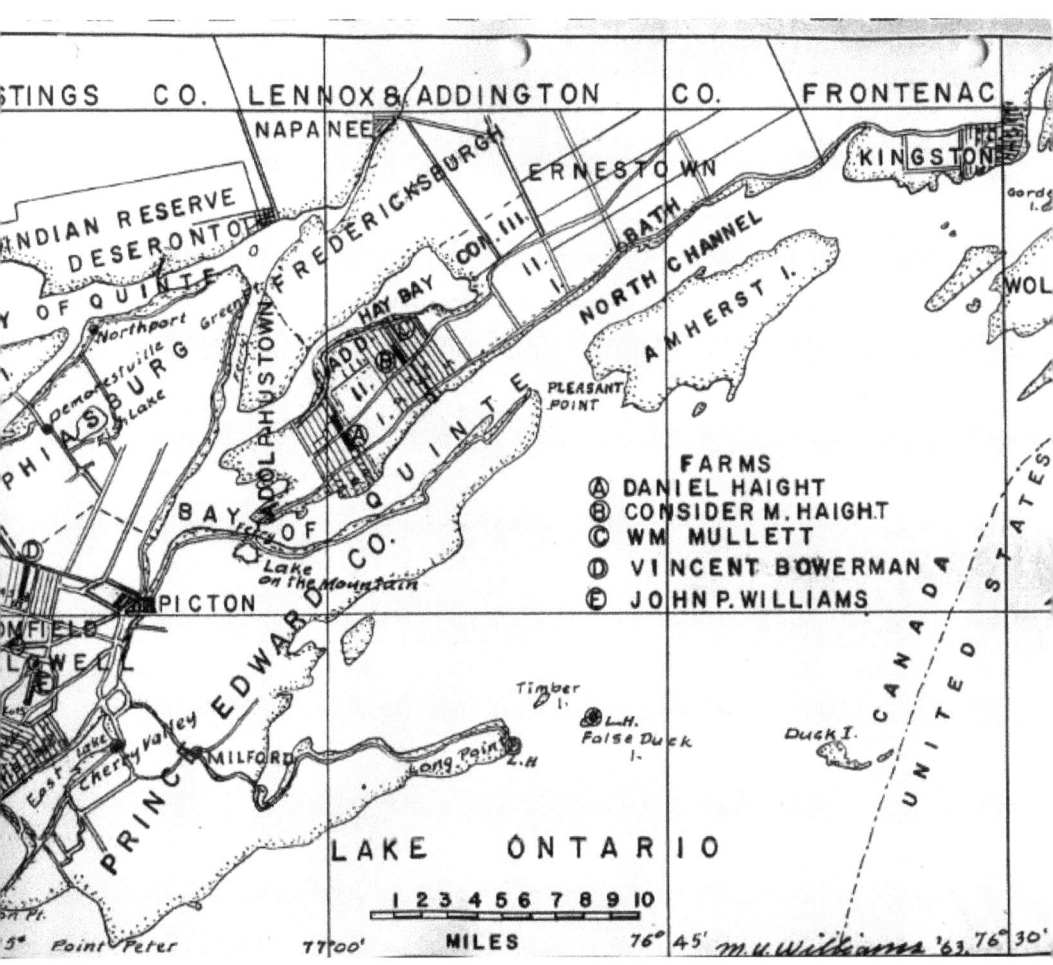

Map of Lennox and Addington County indicating the lot of Daniel Haight.

"Map of Lennox and Addington County," The Canadian County Atlas Digital Project, McGill University, accessed fall 2022,

https://digital.library.mcgill.ca/countyatlas/searchmapframes.php

I do hereby certify that Joel Haight has this day taken the affirmation agreeable to him and is hereby recommended as a proper person to become a settler in this Province given under my name this 27th of July 1797, signed Major Peter Van Alstine, Justice of the Peace. [9]

Joel paid the necessary fee for two hundred acres, fulfilled the requirements, and received his land.

Daniel also received his land grant, and several years later he was able to purchase additional property and build a comfortable colonial home on a two hundred acre farm about three kilometers northeast of the village of Adolphustown.

Comments from Daniel's grandson, Canniff Haight, from his book published in 1899 state:

In 1825–30 the homestead was one of the finest residences in the country. The sketch reproduced for this work was made by Jos. Rolph, Esq., of Toronto, in 1885. The house and barn, as they then appeared, could not be improved. The filling in however, does not represent the place as it used to be. The fence was not circular as shown, and the entrance at the road was broader than it appears. The house faced the west and the driveway brought you round to the south side where was really the principal entrance. In its better days there was a tasty porch over the front door, this, with other things, had disappeared when the sketch was taken, and the old barn which looks so naked, had a large shed on the side next the entrance and also on the opposite side. In the space between the house and barn there was a frame pig-sty, granary and large corn crib. These, with other things, through neglect and decay, have disappeared. [10]

[9] "Results: Land Petitions of Upper Canada, 1763-1865," Library and Archives Canada, Government of Canada, accessed fall 2022, https://www.bac-lac.gc.ca/eng/discover/land/land-petitions-upper-canada-1763-1865/Pages/List.aspx?Surname=Haight&GivenName=Joel&Place=Adolphustown&

For a few years Daniel had a store in Adolphustown, and in 1800 he was appointed clerk of the town. He was a well-read man whose estate included a large collection of books. His grandson, Canniff Haight, recalls Daniel to be "*a man whose sound sense, meekness and probity, had procured for him the respect of all his neighbours and acquaintances. He was a member of the Society of Friends.*" [11] Daniel died in Adolphustown on August 19, 1830, at the age of sixty-six.

Committed to his faith, Daniel never took up arms in any conflict and remained a Loyalist through and through. He lived his life true to his faith, his family and his community.

In 1884, the construction of St. Alban the Martyr Memorial Church began in Adolphustown to commemorate the one hundredth anniversary of the arrival of the United Empire Loyalists. The first service was held on June 25, 1890. The church contains many memorial tiles dedicated to Loyalists and their children. In July 1888, Daniel's grandson, Canniff Haight, purchased and donated a tile in memory of Daniel Haight.

I have had the good fortune of touring this church and the privilege of ringing the bell. After 130 years and with a dwindling congregation, the church closed in 2018. A group of concerned community members formed a registered

[10] Haight, A Genealogical Narrative, 3.

[11] Haight, A Genealogical Narrative, 22.

Dedication Plaque installed in 1884 in St. Alban the Martyr Commemorating the United Empire Loyalists.

"The Neighbourhood Messenger," Adolphustown-Fredericksburgh Heritage Website, Adolphustown-Fredericksburgh Heritage Society, accessed fall 2022, http://www. sfredheritage.on.ca/Newsletter%20Issue%2020%20Apr%202019.pdf

Tile Donated in Memory of Daniel Haight.

St. Alban The Martyr.

charity and they now hold various events throughout the year to raise funds for building maintenance. It is a beautiful church with a number of unique architectural features such as several large stained-glass windows, a vaulted wooden ceiling, and of course the tiles with the names of sixty-four United Empire Loyalists—including Daniel Haight's.

Daniel's decision to move to Upper Canada changed the trajectory of this entire branch of the Haight family. Now proud Canadians, we could easily have been speaking with a New York accent had he not held tight to his convictions and sought a better life for his family.

Quaker Marriages – Adolphustown Community

The Haights quickly established themselves in Adolphustown as an illustrious Quaker family that intermarried with other such families.

Two of Daniel Haight's children married into a prominent English Quaker family, the Mulletts. There were marriages between the Haight and Dorland families, notably between the children of Daniel Haight and Philip Dorland, whose brother, John Dorland, was Daniel's father-in-law.

The branches of this part of the Haight family tree became a bit twisted as stepsiblings married in some instances. Two and three marriages involving blended families can lead to complicated sorting to determine who is who.

Quakers used intermarriage between prominent Quaker families to strengthen both family and faith ties. A second and uniquely gendered strategy among women Friends was the pattern of young Quaker women marrying men outside of the Society of Friends but who lived in the Adolphustown community or surrounding areas. The women later acknowledged their indiscretion in order to be accepted back into membership. It was a matter of "marry first, apologize later." [12]

Although Quakers believed that all were equal, women did not have the same opportunities to leave their communities as men. Women could travel outside their area only if they had permission and it was for religious purposes. Unlike the men who could travel to other areas to seek out a spouse, the women, especially in remote areas like Adolphustown,

---

[12] "The Adolphustown Quakers: Faith, Community, and Marriage Strategies Among the Society of Friends in the Wilderness of Upper Canada," Canadian Friends Historical Association (website), Sydney Harker, accessed fall 2022, cfha.info/journal81p1.pdf

did not have that option.

If a couple wished to marry, their first step was to attend a regular monthly meeting and declare their intentions. They both stood up before the meeting and the man would say "With Divine permission and the Friends' approbation I declare my intention to take this woman (he calls her name) to be my wife." [13] The Society's sanction of the marriage required more than this formality, though. The couple also needed parental consent from each family. Once that was given, a committee of members in good standing was formed to ensure that there were no previous engagements on either side and that they were both members in good standing. Then a final appearance was made before the meeting in which the couple again declared their intentions to marry.

The actual ceremony could take place at a regular meeting or one specially planned. If it was held at a regular meeting, the couple would sit in seats at the front facing the rest of the meeting. Normally the elders would have these seats, but when a couple was to be married, they were to occupy them. The couple would then stand up and marry themselves. The groom would take the brides hand and say, "In the presence of God and this assembly, I take thee to be my wife, promising to be unto thee an affectionate and loving husband until the hand of the Lord by death shall separate us." [14] The bride then repeated the statement.

At the end of the ceremony an elder would speak and then, when there was a pause and if the spirit moved no one else, the meeting would be adjourned. At the close of the meeting, a parchment marriage certificate was brought forward

[13] From an article in British Whig, November 20, 1896.

[14] "Stouffville Free Press (1896) (Stouffville, ON1986), December 4, 1896, p. 6;" OurOntario (website); Ontario Ministry of Tourism, Culture, and Sport; accessed fall 2022; https://news.ourontario.ca/WhitchurchStouffville/details.asp?ID=98051/page/6?n=.

which could be signed by anyone. A special law sanctioned the marriage ceremony. This document, which amounts to the legal sanction of the marriage, is greatly prized among the descendants of Friends.

Quaker Marriage Ceremony

"A Quaker Marriage," Newton Friends Meeting (Quaker Worship in Newtown Pa) (website), Newton Friends Meeting, accessed fall 2022, https://newtownfriendsmeeting.org/committee-pages/care-and-councel-committee/a-quaker-marriage/

A QUAKER WEDDING (LOVE AND LOYALTY).   [by J. Walter West, R.W

Joel Haight—Ninth Generation

Building a Life in Canada

Joel Haight was born about 1770 in Nine Partners, Dutchess, New York. Around 1796, he, along with his uncle, Daniel Haight, and his uncle's family, left New York to settle in Fourth Town (Adolphustown) in Upper Canada.

In December 1797, Joel married Bathsheba Dorland, the daughter of John Dorland and Elizabeth Ricketson. They had seven sons and one daughter: Daniel, Joseph, Thomas, Gilbert, Zachariah, William, Joel, and Margaret.

Like his fourth great grandfather Michael Hoyt, Joel was assigned the position of pound keeper for the township in 1800. Any horses or cattle found running at large within town limits were to be impounded and held. A penalty of poundage fees was payable by the owner.

In 1801, roughly twenty-three per cent of all Adolphustown households identified as Quaker. Joel and Bathsheba's children were admitted to the Adolphustown Meeting of Friends on November 16, 1809.

Bathsheba died at age forty-four in 1819. The following year, Joel requested permission from the Adolphustown Friends Meeting to marry Nancy Ingersoll. Joel and Nancy had one son, Isaac, born in 1822 in Adolphustown.

In 1826, Joel purchased one hundred acres of land (Lot 14, Concession 2) from Joseph Maybee in Adolphustown. Joel grew wheat, which was the main cash crop at the time, with much of it being exported to Britain. Joel's investment in more land to grow wheat proved to be a good business decision. The saying at the time was "wheat bought the farm and barley paid the mortgage."

Joel wrote his will on August 27, 1828, and although the date of his death is uncertain, the records show that the will was probated on March 6, 1829.

The records also indicate that Daniel, Bathsheba, and Joel are among the many Haights buried in the Hay Bay Quaker Cemetery in Adolphustown.

Hay Bay Quaker Cemetery

The plain and simple monuments have only the name of the deceased and their date of death; there are no words of sentiment or poetry. Quakers believe it improper and unpleasant to elevate and celebrate certain people above others through elaborate headstones

Monument Wall, Hay Bay Quaker Cemetery

Haight Burials—Hay Bay Quaker Cemetery

Bathsheba Dorland Haight (September 13, 1774–July 20, 1819) Wife of Joel Haight

Joel Haight (March 17, 1770–1829), husband of Bathsheba Dorland Haight

Consider Merritt Haight Jr (September 20, 1833–November 14, 1834), son of Consider

Consider Merritt Haight (April 28, 1802–May 8, 1838), son of Daniel Haight

Phoebe Haight (September 9, 1831–September 9, 1831), daughter of Consider Haight

Daniel Haight (January 14, 1764–August 19, 1830), husband of Mary Ricketson Dorland

Reuben Amos Haight (February 5, 1800–July 13, 1848), son of Daniel & Mary Ricketson Dorland

Jane West Haight (January 4, 1817–July 15, 1843), wife of Reuben Haight

Mary Ricketson Dorland Haight (March 26, 1771– August 10, 1845), wife of Daniel Haight and sister of Bathsheba Dorland Haight

Shadrick Ricketson Haight (November 22, 1797–June 20, 1840), son of Mary Ricketson Dorland and Daniel Haight

Mary Canniff Haight (February 9, 1802–November 19, 1856), wife of Shadrick Ricketson Haight

Ellen Jane Haight (March 6, 1838–July 28, 1841), daughter of Mary Canniff Haight and Shadrick Ricketson Haight

Mary Elizabeth Haight (November 7, 1834–August 18, 1841), daughter of Mary Canniff Haight and Shadrick Ricketson Haight

Inscription reads "In Memory of Daniel Haight who died Aug. 19. 1830. aged 66 years."

Find a Grave (website), Rocky Sinclair, created January 2, 2013, findagrave.com/memorial/102963706/Daniel-haight #source.

Zachariah Haight—Tenth Generation

Disowned and Reinstated: A Pattern

The next Haight was most likely the black sheep of the family, at least in his own generation.

Zachariah Haight was born in Hallowell, Prince Edward County in Upper Canada into a strong Quaker family, just as the War of 1812 commenced. He was the second youngest child of Joel Haight and Bathsheba Dorland. During this time, many Quakers found themselves caught between the requirements of state policies and religious discipline, both in peace and during war. For Friends, the requirements of duty both to state and to religion led to a collision of opposing principles. As it had during the American Revolution, the Quaker doctrine of pacifism created many problems. Zachariah's parents' and other Quaker community members' neutrality was dictated by their religious beliefs, but it was often interpreted as siding with the enemy.

Hardship continued for Zachariah and his family when his mother died in 1819. He was only seven years old. His father, Joel, married Nancy Ingersoll the following year.

At the age of twenty-nine Zachariah married Sarah Terwilliger, and the couple went on to have four children: Phoebe Jane, Minerva Ann, Thomas Henry, and John William. Sarah was the youngest child of Joseph Terwilliger and Catharina Zufelt, originally from New York. Their ancestors came from the Netherlands and had been in America since the 1600s.

Zachariah and Sarah were married by Reverend James Rogers, a Presbyterian minister. Witnesses were John Arthur and Sarah's brother, William Terwilliger. Sarah was not a member of the Society of Friends and shortly after their marriage, Society of Friends meeting minutes indicate that a complaint was filed against Zachariah. Canada, Quaker Meeting Records 1786–1988 state:

A complaint against Zachariah Haight for keeping company with and marrying a person not of our Society and for neglecting to attend our religious meetings and for not being careful to perform his promises. After deliberation, Arnold Dorland and Jonathan Bowerman were appointed to make him a visit and report to the next meeting. [15]

The Society of Friends have kept meticulous records. It appears that Zachariah was disciplined or disowned and then reinstated more than seventeen times over the years, although not all of his indiscretions were noted. There were no death records located for Sarah, but it appears that Zachariah remarried in about 1863, and another complaint was filed against him for marrying outside the faith. It is assumed that he was once again forgiven. But, twenty years later he was again disowned for an unknown reason.

Zachariah's son, Thomas, also married outside of his faith. Thomas was more than likely disowned as well although he continued to identify as a Quaker until about 1900. At that time, Thomas indicated that he was Methodist, which was the faith of his wife; they were also married in a Methodist church.

In 1871, Zachariah owned twenty-three acres (Lot 9, Concession 3) in Prince Edward County near Bloomfield, Ontario. He grew wheat, corn, potatoes, and apples. He had two cows, ten sheep, and eight pigs, and he also kept bees. He produced one hundred pounds of butter and forty-eight pounds of wool, and at some point, he was also a blacksmith.

---

[15] "West Lake Monthly Meeting (Orthodox) 1828 - 1849," Canadian Friends Historical Association (website), Canadian Friends Historical Association, accessed fall 2022, https://cfha.info/WestLakeO-10-1.pdf

Whether Zachariah was a member in good standing with the Society of Friends or not, the census records throughout his life indicate that he was a Quaker, a fact also stated on his death certificate. Although he may have broken the rules on occasion, it seems that the principles and values of the Quaker religion such as integrity, community, and equality were extremely important to Zachariah during his lifetime— and explains why he continued to identify as a Quaker for his entire life.

Zachariah died of heart failure just before his eighty-eighth birthday in 1900 in Hastings County, Ontario, and he is buried in Prince Edward County, Ontario. Like his grandfather and great grandfather before him he was gifted with a long and fulfilling life.

Quakers, Haights, and the War of 1812 in Upper Canada

During the two-and-a-half-year long War of 1812, Quakers in the United States were persecuted by Americans for being friendly with the British, and in Canada, they were persecuted by the British for being friendly with Americans. For the third time in as many years, the Haights found themselves being judged and punished for their religious beliefs. First, as Puritans in England, then as Quakers during the American Revolution and in Canada for their refusal to participant in the War of 1812. Additionally, the Society of Friends expelled all who bore arms. Most Quakers did not favour one side over the other; they helped anyone who needed it, regardless of who they were.

However, on September 1, 1813, Samuel Haight, a first cousin of Zachariah Haight, made a sworn statement that a neighbour had been aiding and abetting Calvin Wood. Wood supported the Americans and had been charged with treason, jailed, and then freed by the Americans.

Samuel Haight stated that on or about the twentieth day of August 1813, his neighbour had aided and assisted Calvin Wood in cutting and carrying away by force the wheat from a field of a second neighbour. The first neighbour, Moses Terry, was charged with seditious practices which were punishable by execution. Calvin Wood was found guilty of treason, but while being transported to prison, he escaped and was never recaptured.

While the general population was being drafted into the militia in Upper Canada, the Quakers just wanted to be left in peace. But that was not to be, and they were ordered to report for duty. Some men chose to avoid the draft by leaving their homes and going to hide in the wilderness. The British authorities implemented a tax in Upper Canada for those

Battle of the Chateauguay, one of the battles of the War of 1812.

"Battle of the Chateauguay," from lithograph published in Le Journal de Dimanche June 24, 1884, original by Henri Julien CC BY-SA 3.0

individuals who refused to participate in the War of 1812 due to religious convictions. The tax was levied in lieu of combat service. Although Zachariah's father, Joel, and his brother, William, would have been of age to fight, their names do not appear on the list of soldiers.

In Prince Edward County, where Joel Haight's family lived and where his son Zachariah had recently been born, about 160 army officers were ordered to pursue the draft dodgers and jail those that were caught. When a Friend was summoned before a court to answer for his refusal to serve with the militia, he explained that he would rather suffer the penalty of the law than comply with the draft order. The penalty of a tax levy may well have been applied to Joel Haight and other Quakers in his community.

Quakers who served under compulsion were relied on for non-combatant transport and labour duties. Horses that belonged to Quakers were known for their high quality and were commandeered by the military to be used to pull field guns, ammunition, and other material. In some cases, the Quakers concealed their horses, wagons, and harnesses in the woods to avoid accommodating the war effort.

In 1833, warrants of distress were issued against sixty-two Quakers for not having served in the militia during the War of 1812. Finally, in 1849, an act was passed which stated that there would no longer be compulsory service in the militia.

Thomas Henry Haight—Eleventh Generation

Logging for a Living and
Relocation to Cockburn Island

This generation of Haights would soon be on the move, looking for new adventures.

Thomas Henry Haight was born about 1849 in Hallowell, Prince Edward County in Upper Canada. He was the second youngest child of Zachariah Haight and Sarah Terwilliger.

In 1872, Thomas married Mary Alzina Orser, known as Alzina, in the manse of the Methodist Church in Picton, Ontario. In census records, Thomas identified as a member of the Society of Friends.

Alzina's ancestors were from the Netherlands but her branch of the family had been in America since the 1600s. Their surname was originally Aertse before they changed it to Orser once in America. During the American Revolution, because they were loyal to the British Crown, the Orser farms were burned, and assets were stolen. In 1783, the family fled New York for Quebec with the intent of making their way to Upper Canada. Alzina's three times great grandfather, Joseph, was beaten to death by rebels while fleeing. In the fall of 1783, Alzina's great great grandfather Gilbert assisted Deputy Surveyor John Collins with the survey of Township 1, which became Kingston in 1788.

Sometime between 1881 and 1884, Thomas and Alzina, daughter Gertrude, and son Marshall, left Prince Edward County either by ship across Lake Ontario to get to the Erie Canal or by train. They arrived in Grand Rapids, Michigan, where their son, Clarence Adelbert, was born in 1884.

It's interesting to note that Marshall's birth registration states his name as Justin Hanlan Haight. It may have been that they unofficially added the name Marshall after the birth registration because he was known as Marshall or Marsh for his entire life. Incidentally, in March 1903, at the age of twenty-two, Justin Hanlan "Marsh" Haight married eighteen-year-old Millicent "Millie" Maud Ward, daughter of Elias Ward and Leah Playford, and the couple hold the distinction of having the longest marriage to date in the Haight family. In March 1973, the Sault Star acknowledged their seventieth wedding anniversary. The couple was presented with a plaque from Brent Gilbertson, Member of Provincial Parliament, on behalf of then Ontario Premier, William Davis.

Back in the Lower Peninsula of Michigan, we might assume that Thomas worked in the bush as a logger, as forestry workers were very much in demand at that time. By 1870, Michigan was the largest lumber producer in the United States. From about 1869 to 1897, over 160 billion board feet were logged from Michigan forests. Two-hundred-year-old white pine trees were abundant, most being over two hundred feet high and over five feet in diameter. By 1910, the Lower Peninsula of Michigan was a devastated wasteland.

It appears that Thomas and his family only stayed in the area a short time since by 1885 they had made their way from Grand Rapids to Owen Sound, and then by boat to Cockburn Island in Lake Huron, Northern Ontario, where their last child, Stanley Thomas Haight, was born on January 23, 1886. What brought them to this island in the north? The answer lies with the family's connection to the Goodmurphys.

Among the first settlers on Cockburn Island, the Goodmurphys were well established by the time the Haights arrived. Long before the marriage of their children, Stanley Thomas Haight and Clara Belle Goodmurphy, in 1913, there was a connection between the Haights and Goodmurphys. Clara Belle's great grandmother was actually Elizabeth Dorland Haight the granddaughter of Daniel Haight.

Elizabeth's daughter married Solomon Goodmurphy in 1860. Both families came from the same area in Prince Edward County, and both were members of the West Lake Society of Friends (Quakers). Might we assume that the desire to own land and the opportunity to do that on Cockburn Island solidified their decision to settle in the same area?

A towering stack of Michigan timber.

Photo taken between 1880 and 1899. Library of Congress.

"Logging a big load," Library of Congress Prints and Photographs Online Catalog, Library of Congress, accessed fall 2022, http://hdl.loc.gov/loc.pnp/pp.print

The Haights were one of the families to establish a farm in the Scotch Block (the Block) on Cockburn Island. Although fishing and farming (and rumour has it, the odd keg of moonshine) were two of the ways that residents made a living, logging was a key industry on Cockburn Island at this time. In 1898 the province banned the export of raw logs out of the country. This provided a great opportunity for Cockburn Island residents, as sawmills were built to turn the raw logs into merchantable lumber. By about 1904 there were three mills, two in Tolsmaville and one at Ricketts Harbour.

Over the next thirty-five years, the Haights worked hard, and their family grew.

On March 15, 1921, Thomas's wife, Alzina, passed away from heart issues at age seventy-four. That same year, Thomas left Cockburn Island for a farm he had purchased in Little Rapids Village in Thessalon Township. His youngest son, Stanley; daughter-in-law, Clara Belle; and their four children, Carl, Allan, Florence, and Denzil lived with him on the farm.

On February 5, 1925 at age seventy-five, Thomas Henry Haight passed away from heart failure and was buried in Maple Ridge Cemetery, Thessalon, Ontario. Sadly, a year later, Clara Belle, the wife of his son, Stanley, would die of tuberculosis at the age of only thirty—leaving Stanley with four children to raise. It is interesting to note that Clara Belle's mother also died of tuberculosis at the age of thirty-five. It wasn't until 1938, about twelve years after Clara Belle's death, that a vaccine would be available for tuberculosis, sadly, a common disease at the time.

The Haights and the Goodmurphys

We know that there was a connection between the Haight and the Goodmurphy families long before their time on Cockburn Island.

As far back as 1851, the first official census in Upper Canada shows that the Goodmurphy and Haight families were living in Prince Edward County and were all members of the Westlake Society of Friends (Quakers).

The story of the Goodmurphys moving to Canada starts with Lawrence Goodmurphy, the great, great grandfather of Clara Belle. Clara Belle married Stanley Thomas Haight, the youngest son of Thomas Henry Haight. Lawrence was born in Wexford, Ireland and came to Upper Canada sometime after 1823. His son, Soloman, Clara Belle's grandfather, was born in 1839 in the Belleville area and in 1860 married the granddaughter of Daniel Haight. At some point, Soloman and family relocated to Hallowell, Prince Edward County, and Clara Belle's father, Joel, was born there in 1871. They were a well-known family and descendants of the Goodmurphys still live in Prince Edward County today.

It may have been in 1912, when Clara Belle's mother passed away, that she needed a change of scenery and moved to Cockburn Island to live with her aunt and uncle, Henriette and Thomas "Stanley" Goodmurphy. A year later, at the age of seventeen, Clara Belle married Stanley Thomas Haight, nine years her senior, and they began their life together on Cockburn Island. Just thirteen years later, Clara Belle died, leaving her husband and four children behind. Although Stanley and Clara Belle were only married for thirteen years, the connection between the Haights and Goodmurphys spans 170 years.

Lawrence Goodmurphy (1805–1891), Shoemaker - Wexford, Ireland.

"Lawrence Goodmurphy;" WikiTree, Interesting.com Inc.; Patrick Goodmurphy; updated May 21, 2019; wikitree.com/wiki/Goodmurphy-11.

Clarence Adelbert "Del" Haight—Twelfth Generation

Round About Way from Cockburn Island to St. Joseph Island

There had been no Haights from the Joel Haight branch born in the United States since 1770 because Clarence Adelbert Haight's great grandfather and other family members had fled the country in 1796 due to religious persecution. However, things had changed by the time Clarence Adelbert Haight, the son of Thomas Henry Haight and Mary Alzina Orser, was born in Grand Rapids, Michigan, on September 9, 1884.

In this branch of the Haight family, Clarence Adelbert Haight, known as Del, was the last to identify as Quaker, and that was only as a young boy. Later in life, census records indicate that he was Presbyterian. The number of Quakers in Ontario declined from about 7,300 in 1860 to about one thousand during this time period and the Haight's Quaker community all but disappeared. However, the values of hard work and integrity, and their adventurous spirit and ideals remained intact.

After living in Michigan for a short time, the Haights reentered Canada in 1885, and made their way to Cockburn Island. In 1891, we find Adelbert "Del," age six, living with his parents, sister Gertrude (Lena), and brothers Marshall and Stanley on Lot 17, Concession 8 on Cockburn Island. By 1901, the family seems to be well settled. Del is about seventeen; his sister, Gertrude, and brothers, Marshall and Stanley, are living with their parents, Thomas and Alzina, along with Alzina's sister, Hester "Hattie" Orser.

Sometime after 1901, Del relocated to Simcoe County, about three hundred kilometres southeast of Cockburn Island. It was initially thought that he may have gone there to work in the bush. However, research suggests that by that time there was little lumber left, as the area had been cut clean. It's more likely that other work drew him there.

On June 29, 1907, Del married Jessie Amelia Sidey in Toronto Junction in the County of York. The witnesses to their marriage were Jessie's sister, Louisa, and Louisa's husband, Herbert Klopp. Jessie was the daughter of James Sidey and Cordelia Mitchell. Jessie's ancestors hailed from Scotland,

Death Certificate for Jessie Amelia Sidey Haight.

"Ontario Vital Statistics Home Page," Ministry of Public and Business Service Delivery, King's Printer for Ontario, accessed fall 2022, http://www.archives.gov.on.ca/en/tracing/death_registrations.aspx

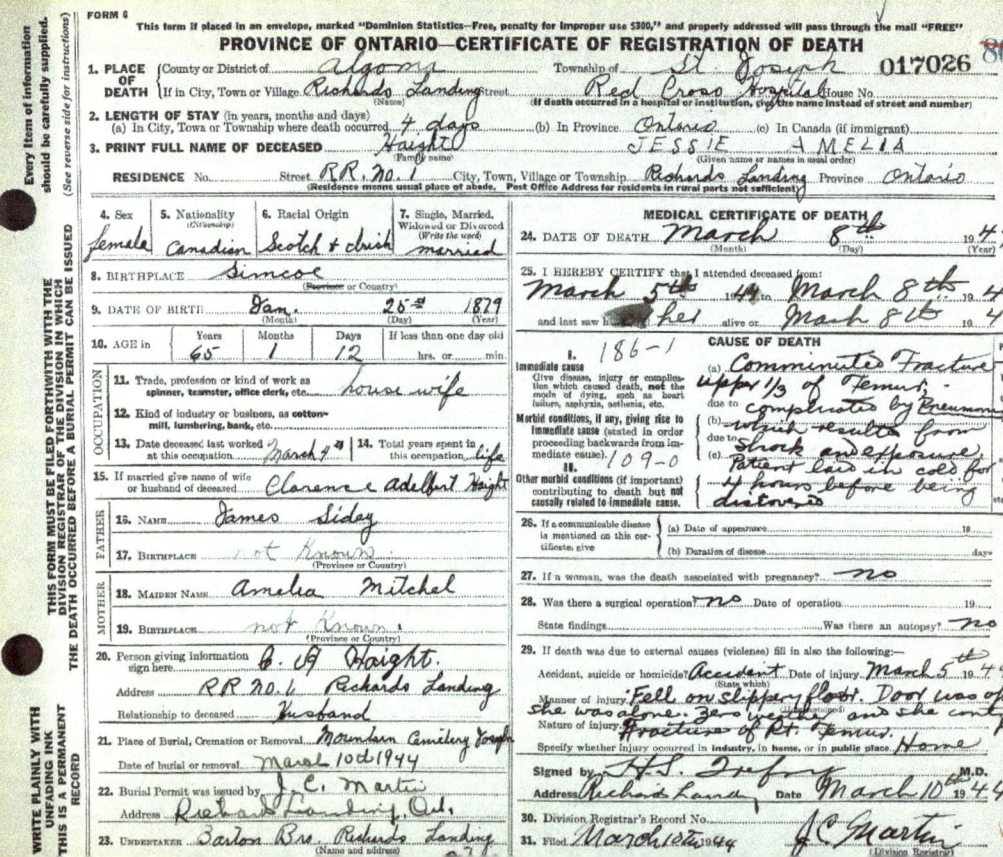

and they settled in Upper Canada in Bewdley, just north of Port Hope.

It appears that Jessie's brother, John Sidey, and his family lived for a time in the Manitoulin area of Ontario, so it could be that the families knew one another prior to Del and Jessie's marriage. Jessie's brother was living in the Creemore area around the time Del moved there, so perhaps having acquaintances in the area was a reason for Adelbert's relocation.

After their marriage, Del and Jessie moved to Cockburn Island. They lived with Thomas and Alzina on Lot 17, Concession 8 and on April 24, 1908, their first son, Walter Stanley, was born. On November 11, 1912, Del purchased one hundred acres (Lot 20 on Concession 8) from Joseph Matthews, a resident of St. Clair, Michigan. Until this time, Del had been working for one of the logging companies and helping his father, Thomas, on his farm. Now he had a farm of his own; however, as most men did on Cockburn Island, he continued to work in the bush during the winter months.

On May 17, 1914, their second son, Randall James Thomas, was born and on January 7, 1917, their third son, Benjamin Franklin, was born.

After World War I, Cockburn Island's logging industry was in decline. The year 1921 seems to have been pivotal for some families. Change was in the air as some families left to find work and better opportunities elsewhere. Del's mother had passed away and his father moved to Thessalon. It was at this time that Del and his family moved back to Simcoe County where they owned a six-room house and farm near Creemore. They were in Simcoe County when their sister-in-law, Clara Belle, died of tuberculosis.

By 1930, Del, Jessie, and family were on the move again. In April 1930, Del purchased a farm on 10th Side Road (known as

Poverty Hill) on St. Joseph Island in Northern Ontario. It was Lot 11, Concession M, Jocelyn Township. In 1934, Del, Jessie, and sons Walter and Randall were living on the farm. Ben, about eighteen, had already left home. In 1935, Walter, the eldest son, married Sarah Delena Winnifred Smith and they took over the farm. Del and Jessie purchased another farm on the Hilton Road where the current All Tribes Christian Camp is located.

On March 5, 1944, tragedy struck while Jessie was at home alone. She slipped on a wet floor, fell, and broke her femur. The door was open and let in the cold; she was not discovered until four hours later. Jessie developed pneumonia from shock and exposure and died on March 8, 1944, at the age of sixty-five.

Eight months after his wife Jessie's death, Del married Pearl McCaig, who had been born on Cockburn Island to Archibald McCaig and Jennie Gilbert. Pearl was the aunt of Del's daughter-in-law, Thelma McCaig. Prior to her marriage, Pearl had been diagnosed as a typhoid carrier—a diagnosis she did not reveal to her new husband and family. She had been instructed by the public health department to keep them advised of her whereabouts. Unfortunately, she did not heed these instructions and infected Walter and Sarah's daughter, Donna. This did not go over well with the Haight family and it appears that Del sent Pearl packing.

In December 1954 at the age of seventy, Clarence Adelbert Haight passed away and was buried in the Mountain Maple Grove Cemetery on St. Joseph Island alongside his first wife, Jessie Amelia Sidey. Like his forebearers, he had courage and an adventurous spirit, and he moved his family several times to improve their circumstances.

Walter Stanley Haight—Thirteenth Generation

From the Mountain to the Twin Lakes

This was a close-knit family with Walter's grandparents, Thomas and Alzina, living nearby along with his aunt and uncle, Millie and Marshall. Working in the bush as well as farming kept the family sustained, although it wasn't an easy life. Walter and his brothers, Randall and Ben, worked alongside their parents on the farm. Every family member had chores: they had to milk the cows, gather eggs, clean the outhouse, wash clothes, fill the wood box, and work in the

Walter Stanley Haight is the eldest son of Clarence Adelbert Haight and Jessie Amelia Sidey. He was born on Cockburn Island on April 24, 1908.

fields and bush. They made do with what they had and were thankful.

Family and friends supported one another on this small and isolated island. Home, school, and church were the heart of the community. They enjoyed concerts, meetings, square dances, and other social events. Gatherings included lots of music with neighbours (including Marsh Haight and Arthur Pateman) on the fiddle providing entertainment.

Music in the Genes

Music played an important part in the lives of early settlers. They brought their music, songs, and dances with them to their new home. It was a great source of enjoyment and entertainment whether at church, school concerts, dance halls, or in someone's kitchen on a cold winter's night. Researchers say that musical ability is 50 percent inherited. The Haights seemed to have a natural ear for music and were self-taught in the early days. Usually it began with singing in church or at home around the piano or organ. There is a thread of violin and fiddle playing in the Haight family that wends its way back to the earliest days. The Haights were also known to call the odd square dance. They had great vocals and performed at local seniors' homes, fairs, concerts, and dances.

"We learned to sing in church," recalled Donna Haight Hadden, daughter of Walter and Sarah Haight.

I ordered a piano course on records and taught myself to begin with. Much practice and determination got me to where I am. I chorded on the old pump organ we had at home. Billy made me play for his guitar and violin practicing. You pumped like crazy, pulled all the stops out, and tried to keep up to him. One day, after I was married, a delivery truck arrived at our little house at the Twin Lakes with a used piano from Eatons. I told them that I hadn't bought a piano, but upon surveying the receipt I found that it was my mother-in-law Winnie Hadden who had purchased the piano for me as a gift. I played the piano in Richards Landing Hall with Billy and Johnny Richardson and also at the Dew Drop Inn with Fred Kent's band on occasion. Billy and Glenda couldn't sing harmony. I recall Billy saying that he didn't have a clue. Glenda chorded on the piano, guitar, and autoharp. I chorded on the autoharp and the piano when I sometimes played with Billy at dances. I played for years at the Free Methodist Church on the Island. We all had a natural ear for music and used our talent often, so people asked us to sing at lots of functions.

The tradition continues with some of the great grandchildren of Walter Stanley Haight who are now classically trained, talented musicians and teachers.

Walter Stanley Haight—Thirteenth Generation

As mentioned before, sometime before June 1921, Del, Jessie, and family (including Walter) left Cockburn Island and returned to Sunnidale Township in Simcoe County where Jessie's relatives, the Sidey family, lived and where Jessie had been born and raised. Here they purchased a farm with a six-room house. Jessie's brother, Albert, lived with them and helped on the farm.

For the next nine years, the Haights farmed and took on odd jobs to make a living.

When Walter was twenty-two, his father moved the family to a farm on St. Joseph Island on what was known as Poverty Hill. Five years later on July 25, 1935, Walter married Sarah Delena Winnifred Smith, the daughter of George Andrew Torrie Smith and Mary Delena May Bookman, who were neighbours living just down on the Hilton Road. Sarah's son, Wilfred George "Billy or Bill," joined the Haight family. The same year that they got married, Walter and Sarah took over the farm on Poverty Hill.

Walter and Sarah's daughter, Donna Lorene, was born on January 26, 1936 in the hospital in Richards Landing. The snow was so deep that year that on the way home Walter had to walk alongside the cutter to prevent it from tipping over with mother and baby on board.

Over the years, Walter had developed an interest and some expertise with horses. His knowledge proved useful on the farm and elsewhere, and it always ensured that the horses were well looked after and treated kindly. Walter was quoted as saying:

"A man cannot get as much work out of a horse that has sore shoulders as he can from one with sound shoulders. The same

is true for their feeding, shelter, and protection from flies, etc., and besides all this, there is the moral and spiritual benefit derived from a mind and heart humanely educated."

This was a philosophy founded in Walter's Puritan and Quaker roots.

Walter's daughter, Donna, recalls that he didn't own a tractor for many years but he always had a good team of horses.

Walter was one of the founders and an inspector for the St. Joseph Island Humane Society from 1939 until about 1964. He investigated complaints and randomly dropped into various

Walter's horse, Tony, who weighed in at about two thousand pounds and who was used to help clear timber at the Twin Lakes.

farms to ensure that the animals were properly cared for. In 1953, Walter's name was put forward to the Ontario Society for the Prevention of Cruelty to Animals so that he could become an inspector in the bush camps on the North Shore. He was very concerned that the loggers were using the wrong-sized collars which would cause sores, and he knew that the horses' hooves were often neglected. He taught the men how to fit the collars and how to maintain the horses' hooves properly.

On Valentine's Day, February 14, 1938, Walter Lyle Haight was born. Eighteen months passed, and on August 28, 1939, Walter and Sarah's daughter, Glenda Marilyn, was born. Only one month later, Canada declared war on Germany—the Second World War had begun.

Cash was not a plentiful commodity in the 1930s and 1940s. During the Great Depression and World War II, the Haight

Twin Lakes, St. Joseph Island, Ontario.

family had to manage with what they had. They canned everything—including meat. They had a root cellar for vegetables; a cow for milk, butter, and cream; and chickens for meat and eggs. This ensured that there was always food on the table. Blueberry picking was a family adventure, and it guaranteed that you would be rewarded with a piece of pie. Sarah Haight was well known for her pastry and she was an exceptional cook. Repair, reuse, make-do, and don't throw anything away. That was the motto during those years. Socks were mended, patches were sewn over holes, clothing was made from flour sacks, and homemade knitted mitts and socks were the order of the day.

In 1956, Walter purchased a property on St. Joseph Island. The property was on Hilton Road and was called the Twin Lakes. It is the largest lake on the island, and at the time it was undeveloped with large stands of timber. Walter purchased it from the estate of Lieutenant Colonel Cary Ingram Crockett, who was a distant relative of the famed Davy Crockett, and whose father and stepfather had been Confederate soldiers of distinction during the American Civil War. We have no idea why Lt. Col. Crockett would purchase this little piece of heaven, the Twin Lakes, or how he even knew of its existence since he was working and living in Manila in the Philippines when he acquired the property. The property was held by his estate until 1956, when Walter purchased it for $2,000.

In September 1957, Walter sold the farm on Poverty Hill that he and Sarah and their family had lived in for twenty-two years; the couple moved to a house at the Twin Lakes while they built a new home on an adjoining lot.

In 1961, Walter submitted for approval a plan for the Haight Subdivision at the Twin Lakes. This was also the beginning of the Twin Lakes Campground, which was a very successful venture that Walter and Sarah ran for many years.

Not one to rest on his laurels, Walter was also the road

superintendent for Hilton Township, he sat on the board of the Mountain Maple Grove Cemetery, he was president of the St. Joseph Island Corn Growers Association, and he was a director with the local chamber of commerce. He drove a school bus, he delivered the mail for Hilton Township, and he was an inspector for the humane society. Sarah, although not well for many years, delivered mail, taught Sunday school, participated in church committees, and worked alongside Walter in running the campsite.

It was on Sunday, January 19, 1969, that tragedy struck. On that night, Sarah's mother, Mary Bookman Smith, Sarah's sister, Marie, and her sister's husband, Laurence Rains, were all visiting with Walter and Sarah at the home that they had built at the Twin Lakes. Suddenly, it became apparent that there was a fire in the house. It was later determined that it had started in the attic. It was well underway before it was discovered. The telephone wires were destroyed which made it impossible to call for help. Luckily, everyone escaped the house, but by the time the fire department arrived, the house was fully engulfed.

Walter and Sarah lost everything in the fire and went to live with Marie and Laurence for the remainder of the winter. In the spring they purchased a mobile home and had it installed at the Twin Lakes site.

In 1972, when Walter and Sarah were in their early sixties, they sold the Twin Lakes and moved to a newly built apartment building in Hilton Beach. It was a difficult adjustment for Walter and it put to the test the independence and tenacity that were so deeply seated in his genes. Until now he had had a home and land to take care of and the ability to do as he pleased. He wasn't accustomed to following a landlord's rules. The building had a "no pets" policy and Walter owned a dog. Just prior to the building's grand opening, when several dignitaries would be in attendance, it was suggested that Walter keep the dog inside his apartment and not make it known that he had a pet. As the invited guests toured the building, Walter suggested to the dignitaries that they tour his apartment but "Be careful you don't let the dog out when you open the door." Well, that secret was no secret anymore. He was going against the rules and the dog had to go; this broke Walter's heart. Walter and Sarah's son, Bill, agreed to take the dog.

In the winter Walter strung an extension cord over their balcony and across the parking lot so that he could plug in his car, and he mounted bird feeders on two-by-fours on the balcony, but these things were also against the rules. Walter tried to push the envelope at every turn, and he always kept the building manager on his toes.

Although she was ill for most of her adult life, barely able to walk, and hospitalized numerous times over the years, Sarah always remained positive no matter how much pain and discomfort she felt. She was a devout Christian and lifelong member of the Free Methodist Church on St. Joseph Island, and her faith and family gave her the strength and fortitude to carry on and outlive the three doctors who advised her to prepare for her death.

For the occasion of Sarah's sixty-fifth birthday, her son, Bill, penned this poem:

Mother

Today is my mother's birthday

And I just don't know where to start

To find a gift that would show her

The way that I feel in my heart

What gift could I buy that would tell her

How I miss those old days at home

On the old farm up on the mountain

Picking potatoes and stones

To me she was nurse and companion

A friend when I needed to talk

She even took time to go fishing

When so tired she hardly could walk

She helped me with chores and my homework

And those other odd jobs on the farm

Then sit up half the night and knit mittens

In winter to keep my hands warm

She has given so much in her lifetime

And she taught me the good from the bad

She listened while I practiced the fiddle

T'would have driven anybody else mad

So God let me say "Happy Birthday"

Give her peace, give her love, give her joy

And give her the love and compassion

That she gave to her little boy

Written by Bill Haight, 1975

On December 19, 1979, at age sixty-nine, Sarah closed her eyes for the final time. She had lived her life well, raised a family, and been blessed with eleven grandchildren; she was at peace.

In 1980, Walter married Beatrice Annie Netherton, and they

continued to live in the apartment in Hilton Beach.

On April 8, 1981, just shy of his seventy-third birthday, Walter Stanley Haight passed away. He was buried alongside Sarah in the Mountain Maple Grove Cemetery on St. Joseph Island. His humble beginnings on a farm where he had worked alongside his father and where he had been surrounded by his tightly knit community had led to deeply engrained values and a long history of animal advocacy. He had not taken kindly to interference from others, and he had been inclined to be intolerant of those who could not use common sense. He was not a church-going man, but he did, however, inherit some of the Haight characteristics of his ancestors—most arguably of which was his tenacity. At his funeral service held on April 11, 1981, at the Free Methodist Church on St. Joseph Island, Reverend Ralph Byggdin spoke of this. He said, "If Walter came upon a mountain, he would use all his power and might to climb it. If that failed, Walter would simply plow right through it."

The Haight Women

Although this book focuses on the male descendants of the Haight family, we mustn't forget that there were generations of women who worked and walked alongside these men, and who shared in all their triumphs, tragedies, and accomplishments.

Their sacrifice and fortitude have contributed to the character and strength of the descendants that followed. Isolation, deprivation, and hardship turned to persistence, optimism, resourcefulness, and the acceptance of hard work. Their circumstances would have probably crushed a

Walter and Sarah Haight on the occasion of their fortieth wedding anniversary in 1975.

modern person, but to them it was the day-to-day reality of life. Some came from established towns and villages with money and possessions to a desolate wilderness where they had to clear land, build a home, and raise and feed their families. Others came with barely the clothes on their backs. They were hoping for a better life, escaping persecution, and looking for the opportunity to own their own land. Simon Hoyt's wife, Susannah, had to set up a home several times in various locations while supporting and raising a family. This enabled her husband to establish towns and villages in Massachusetts and Connecticut.

These women were willing to do whatever it took to make life better for their families. Many died in childbirth at a young age or from illnesses that we don't often hear about today—other than in the history books. Joseph Haight's wife, Mary Anne Palmer, a mother of seven children, died at the age of thirty-nine, leaving three of her children under the age of ten. Cholera, childbirth, smallpox, flu, measles, and tuberculosis were just some of the maladies that caused their demise. An example was Clara Belle Goodmurphy, the wife of Stanley Haight, who died at the age of thirty from tuberculosis. There were few doctors and no vaccines or medicines available. Should they die prematurely, it was very common for their husbands to remarry shortly afterwards so that there was someone there to raise the children. Six of the Haight men in our story married a second time after the deaths of their first wives.

In all, there were ninety children born to these women—most during very difficult times. They were industrious, hardworking women, and they were pillars of their families, churches, and communities; they are owed enormous gratitude from the generations that followed.

It is also of note that Haight women, as members of the West Lake Society of Friends in Prince Edward County, were instrumental in working to assist slaves in the United

States and to support freed slaves in Upper Canada. They were committed to the cause of abolition long before the organization of formal anti-slavery societies in Canada. They worked tirelessly to raise money to send to their religious connections in the United States to help those Americans in their ongoing efforts to abolish slavery. As well, the West Lake Society women helped slaves escape to freedom in Upper Canada. Between 1840 and 1860, run-away slaves from America crossed over the border in their search for a safe place. Travelling the so-called Underground Railway was a secretive and dangerous venture. There was a strong Quaker network that supported the operation of safe houses that were located in between the settlements of Pickering, Niagara, Newmarket, and the Bay of Quinte.

These women were certainly not fragile but were full of courage, determination, and fortitude. They were devoted to their beliefs in a righteous cause and were ever present to guard, comfort, and love their families.

Susannah North Martin (1621–1692).

Other Kin

Some would like to believe that they descend from royalty or someone famous. Most of our ancestors were simply ordinary folks who did some extraordinary things. Although they were not direct Haight descendants, these individuals embodied the true characteristics of the Haight's: courage, tenacity, vision, and purpose.

Susannah North Martin was executed by hanging on June 29, 1692, during the Salem witch trials.

When I had visited Salem, Massachusetts and the Salem Witch Museum several years ago, I had no idea of the connection between these legendary and historical events and the Haight family. I must admit that I was fascinated by this discovery. I am reminded however, that these were real people caught up in this hysteria—ones who genuinely feared the devil's presence in their lives.

The belief in witches goes back to the fourteenth century in Europe. Those that came to the Massachusetts Bay Colony in the seventeenth century brought those beliefs and fears with them. There have been many theories over the years as to what caused the witch craze, and one of the more prominent is the competition between Catholics and Protestants. We already know how the Puritans felt about the Catholic Church. Women were more often accused of being witches as they were thought to be weaker and more prone to be influenced by the devil. Every natural disaster or human misfortune in those years was automatically attributed to witchcraft. Witches could inflict disease, spoil crops, cause bad weather, and bring about the stillbirth of livestock (not to mention many other calamities).

Susannah North is a descendant of Thomas Hoyt's (first generation) daughter Mary Hoyt. She was born on September 30, 1621, in Buckinghamshire, England to Richard North and

Joan Bartram. Her family moved to Salisbury, Massachusetts, which was part of the Massachusetts Bay Colony, in around 1639 when Susannah was about eighteen years old. In 1646, Susannah married a widower and blacksmith, George Martin, and together they had eight children.

Life for Susannah in the Massachusetts Bay Colony, as it was in general for most women during the seventeenth century, was difficult. She, like all women of that time, had no religious or legal rights (which were essentially one and the same in Puritan society). Susannah's legal identity was taken over by her husband when she married. Women were believed to be incapable and sinful by nature.

As a good wife, Susannah was expected to provide her husband with material, spiritual, and emotional comforts. In addition, she would bear children, raise them, maintain the household, assist with planting and harvesting, and whenever necessary brand steers and tend to cattle—all the while being obedient to her husband and a model wife.

Over the years, Susannah gained a reputation as forthright and argumentative which was not acceptable for a woman in Puritan society. She was viewed by her neighbours as a troublemaker, and was even charged for calling out one of her neighbours as a liar and a thief. She was no stranger to the courts as well, having pursued six unsuccessful attempts regarding the inheritance of her father's estate.

She was accused of witchcraft on two occasions prior to 1692 with the charges eventually being dropped. In the first case, she was accused by William Browne of tormenting his wife Elizabeth with her spirit and driving her insane. In the second case, in 1669, William Sargent said that he witnessed Susannah give birth to and kill an illegitimate baby. Considering that she was forty-eight years old at the time, this seemed very unlikely. The charges were eventually dropped, and Susannah's husband, George, later sued Mr.

Sargent for slander.

In 1686 Susannah's husband, George, died. This left Susannah a poor and defenseless widow. She had no financial means, and because this was a patriarchal society, Susannah had no one to support or protect her. The community obviously had no sympathy for her, and the gossip about her and the general dislike for her continued. Simmering tensions would be fueled by the suspicions and resentment of her neighbours.

In 1692, two men named Susannah a witch and stated that she had attempted to recruit them into witchcraft. She was also accused by another man who claimed that she had bewitched his oxen and driven them into the river where they drowned. On April 30 of that year, several young girls, represented by two men, claimed that she had bewitched them.

It's interesting to note that the accusers did not live in Susannah's village, and they didn't even know her personally. It is suspected that these girls may have heard of Susannah's perceived bad reputation from others and then made the decision to accuse her, perhaps to achieve some form of personal notoriety. Susannah was escorted the twenty miles to Salem Village where she was questioned and where she twice underwent the humiliating physical examination to find her "witches mark."

No such mark was found. She proved by all accounts to be pious, and she quoted the Bible freely— something a witch was said to be incapable of doing. During the judge's questioning, the young accusers were writhing on the floor and contorting, and they appeared to be having "fits." Susannah was sent to Boston to be held there until her trial.

In May she was transported from Boston to Salem and on June 26, 1692, her trial began. She was denied any legal representation. At least nine of her neighbours made the trip to Salem to relate the damage that she had done to them over the years such as casting spells and causing them harm. Even her personal neatness was taken as proof of devotion to the devil.

Susannah did not help her defence by laughing at the accusations made against her. She stated that she led a most virtuous and holy life. She refused to be intimidated by her accusers. When the judge asked for her opinion about what afflicted the young girls, Susannah suggested that they might be the ones under the influence of the devil—not her.

Reverend Cotton Mather, a well-respected Puritan minister stated, "I believe this woman to be one of the most impudent, scurrilous, wicked creatures in the world." Susannah mounted a vigorous defence, but she was found guilty of witchcraft. The court met again on June 29 and despite the lack of evidence against her, the judge sentenced Susannah along with Sarah Good, Sarah Wildes, Elizabeth Howe, and Rebecca Nurse to death by hanging.

Although Reverend Cotton Mather's opinion of Susannah certainly did not help her situation nor prevent her execution, he did try to warn the judges that testimony based on dreams and visions, and not on actual hard evidence was wrong. However, his concerns were ignored. It wasn't until the trials began to lose support that the court admitted their mistake and in 1697, they deemed the trials unlawful.

The lead justice Samuel Sewall publicly apologized for his role. The damage to the community lingered even after legislation was passed that restored the names of the condemned. In May 1693 all those charged and imprisoned were pardoned and released. In all, twenty individuals were hanged for witchcraft during the infamous trials.

[16] "Susannah Martin House Marker," Salem Witch Museum, accessed fall 2022, https://salemwitchmuseum.com/locations/susannah-martin-house-marker/

Monument Salem Massachusetts. In Memory of the Innocent Victims of the Salem Witch Trials.

"Salem Village Witchcraft Victims' Memorial," The Historical Marker Database, photograph by Bill Coughlin (April 16, 2009), accessed fall 2022, https://www.hmdb.org/PhotoFullSize.asp?PhotoID=61555

Canniff Haight (1825–1901). Courtesy of Toronto Public Library Digital Archive, 2021.

Canniff Haight, Country Life in Canada Fifty Years Ago (Hunter, Rose and Company,1885).

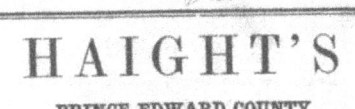

HAIGHT'S
PRINCE EDWARD COUNTY
ALMANAC,
FOR THE YEAR OF OUR LORD,
1855.

"A NIMBLE SIXPENCE IS BETTER THAN A SLOW SHILLING."

PUBLISHED BY C. HAIGHT.
PICTON, C.W.

Haight's Almanac, published by Canniff Haight.

Canadiana (website), Canadian Research Knowledge Network, accessed fall 2022, canadiana. ca/view/oocihm.8_ 00365_1/1.

In 1711, the Massachusetts legislature passed a resolution clearing the names of the convicted witches and offered financial restitution to their descendants. Susannah's family did not wish to be named in the law and did not seek restitution. In 1894 the residents of Amesbury where Susannah had lived placed a stone marker near Susannah and George's home that read:

Here stood the house of Susannah Martin. An honest, hardworking Christian woman accused of being a witch and executed at Salem, July 29, 1692. She will be missed! A Martyr of Superstition [16]

In 1957, the Massachusetts legislature formally apologized to the victims but it did not specifically mention any of them by name. In 1992, the Salem Witch Trials Memorial was built in Salem and a marker was established for Susannah Martin. In 2001, the Massachusetts legislature passed a resolution which officially exonerated five of the victims—one of whom was Susannah North Martin. In 2017, the Proctor's Ledge Memorial was built in Salem and a marker was established for Susannah.

Susannah North Martin's characteristics certainly encompassed those mentioned at the 1866 Hoyt reunion. Her tenacity to cling to her opinions, and her courage, conviction, and faith were ever present throughout her life. However, the fear and superstitions of others caused her to lose her life despite her fortitude. It has been over three hundred years since these horrific events, and it is still talked about today. Let's remember Susannah for standing up for what she believed and for not allowing herself to be influenced by others. May she rest in the peace that she so seldom knew in life.

Canniff Haight was the grandson of Daniel Haight and Mary Dorland. He was well-educated, and was a druggist, bookseller, and author. He made his living as a farmer,

Frederick Maxfield Hoyt (1873–1940).

"Frederick Maxfield Hoyt;" Find a Grave (website); Friends of Cedar Lawn, Jeff Record; added September 20, 2008; findagrave.com/memorial/29948774/frederick-maxfield-hoyt.

P.T. Barnam (1810–1891).

"P. T. Barnum" by Harvard Library, Public Domain (author's life plus seventy years)

merchant, librarian, and scholar. He was the author of Country Life in Canada Fifty Years Ago, which was published in 1885, and from which I was able to glean information and many interesting facts about the Haight family. He was also the author of A Genealogical Narrative of the Daniel Haight Family, published in 1899, and A United Empire Loyalist in Great Britain (subtitled Here and There in the Homeland) published in 1895. He also authored other books, and he was the publisher of Haight's Prince Edward County Almanac. He became a Loyalist cataloguer in the United States Library of Congress.

Frederick Maxfield Hoyt, a descendant of Simon Hoyt, was born in Stamford, Connecticut in 1873. He graduated from Yale in 1895, shortly before marrying Jane Ann Forby. He was a senior partner for the Lace Importing Company. He and his wife boarded the RMS Titanic in Southampton as first-class passengers, with their destination being Stamford, Connecticut. During the legendary and tragic sinking of the great liner, Frederick escorted his wife to collapsible Lifeboat D. Frederick would eventually jump from the ship and be pulled into a lifeboat. They were rescued by the RMS Carpathia and thus became two of the lucky survivors of one of history's worst maritime disasters.

Phineas Taylor Barnam, the co-founder of the famous Barnum and Bailey Circus, was a direct descendant of Simon Hoyt, his fifth great grandfather. He was also an author, publisher, and philanthropist. Although there is no evidence, it has been said that he coined the phrase "There's a sucker born every minute." He served two terms in the Connecticut legislature, the first in 1865 just after the Civil War ended, and the second in 1866; both times were as a Republican for Fairfield, Connecticut. He was elected mayor of Bridgeport, Connecticut in 1875. He did not start his circus business until he was sixty years old, but the circus is what he is generally remembered for.

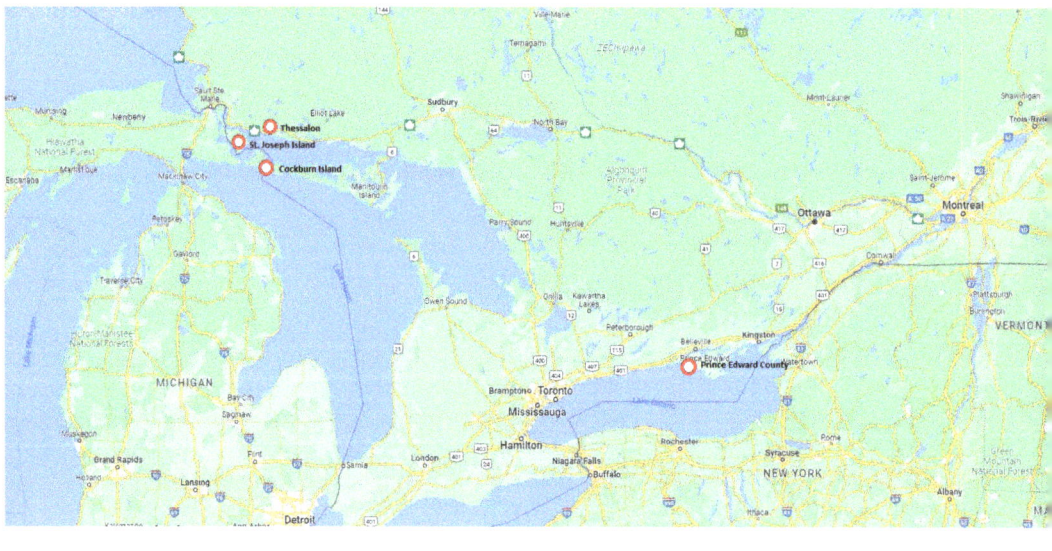

Locations where the Haights settled over the years—Prince
Edward County, Cockburn Island, Thessalon, and St. Joseph
Island.

PART II | Places

Home Sweet Home

The Haight's have been in Canada and more especially Ontario for well over three hundred years. Persecuted in England and the United States for their religious beliefs, they found that Canada welcomed them, and it is here that they made their home and where they continue to live today.

Haight descendants of today are very nostalgic about their personal pasts, with strong attachments to the places, farms, and families of past generations. Memories of childhood adventures while growing up bring us back to simpler times: houses lit by coal oil lamps, the smell of fresh baked apple pie, and the taste of homemade bread. As the fire crackles in the woodstove, we listen to stories read from the Family Herald. These things call us back to Prince Edward County, Cockburn Island, and St. Joe.

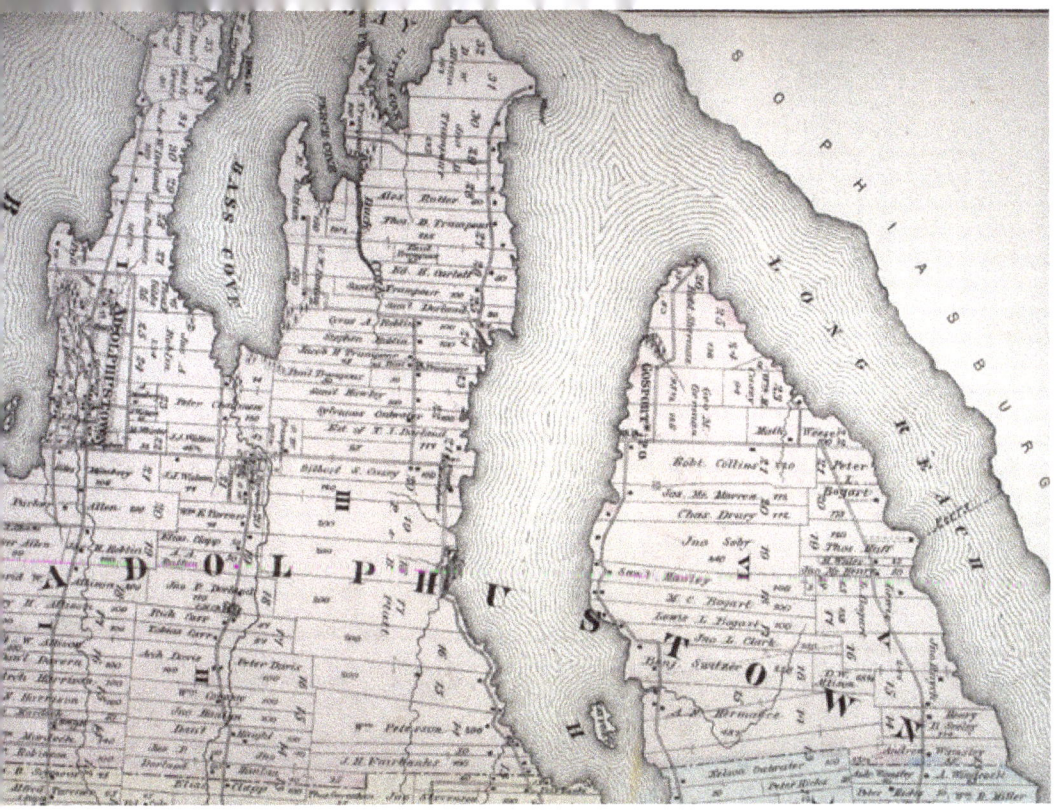

Adolphustown in Lennox and Addington County.

The Canadian County Atlas Digital Project, Rare Books and Special Collections, McGill University Library, Montreal (2001)

Island Life in Canada

Although Adolphustown, where the first Haights arrived in Upper Canada, is not an island, it is surrounded by water on three sides with the Bay of Quinte and the Napanee River defining most of its borders.

Cockburn Island and St. Joseph Island, where later descendants settled, are islands located in the northwestern part of Lake Huron. Cockburn Island is separated from the westernmost point of Manitoulin Island by the Mississagi Strait and from Michigan's Drummond Island by the False Detour Channel. St. Joseph Island sits near the mouth of the St. Mary's River. Both Cockburn Island and St. Joseph Island are part of the Manitoulin chain of islands.

There is no question that life for an early settler was difficult, but trying to eke out a living on an isolated island was all the more challenging. The Haights were not daunted, though, by the hard work and struggles that they knew they would experience in order to establish their farms and eventually thrive.

In 1783, a band of Loyalists under the command of Captain Van Alstine left New York with a fleet of seven sailing ships. They were heading for Quebec where they would spend the winter. In May 1784, a brigade of bateaux (flat bottomed, shallow-draft boats) left Quebec and reached Adolphustown on June 16.

The new arrivals pitched their tents and, surrounded by their meager belongings, set about drawing for the lots upon which they would build their homes. Since the township was surrounded by water on three sides, lots along the shore were the most prized as there were no roads, and the only mode of travelling at that time was water. Easy access to it for other uses such as watering cattle and crops as well land near water also tends to be more fertile. Daniel and Joel Haight arrived in Adolphustown in about 1796.

Two generations later, in 1885, Thomas and Alzina Haight, along with their children Gertrude, Marshall, and Clarence Adelbert Haight, landed on the shores of Cockburn Island. The island had been surveyed in 1878 and a township formed in 1881. Settlers, who were mostly fishermen, had arrived prior to 1878 and had already established themselves. But there was still plenty of work to be done for those arriving in 1880 and afterward.

By the time Thomas Haight and his family arrived, many of the lots had been partially cleared. One of those areas, and the place where the Haights made their home, was the

Scotch Block. It was about five kilometers from the village of Tolsmaville. There were already several families living in that area including the Goodmurphys. These current residents did mixed farming and in the winter they cut timber.

Thirty-five years later, in 1921, Clarence Adelbert "Del" Haight and his family made their way from Cockburn Island to Creemore, and in 1930 from there to St. Joseph Island where the family remained for nearly seventy seven years. The farm they purchased had been established over thirty years before and had a good solid house, outbuildings, an orchard, and cleared land for crops and pasture.

The unique challenges of island life were met head-on by our ancestors. Their resilience should remind us of the privileges that we have acquired, while we still recognize that our family came from humble beginnings. They were cut-off from civilization for several months of the year while they waited for the ice to come in or go out. This meant that there was no mail and no outside communications during this time. Their isolated lifestyle also meant that, before the winter started, they had to ensure that the root cellar was full, and sufficient wood was cut, split, and dried in order to tide them over until the spring. Our ancestors were certainly a resilient bunch, taking isolation and the need for self-sufficiency all in stride. That day in the spring when the first ship arrived with the mail and much needed supplies was one of excitement and celebration.

Perils of the Waters

Since the only modes of transportation were water or ice, there were many calamities and deaths over the years. In 1816, the Kingston Chronicle reported that a scow crossing from Adolphustown had sunk. There had been eleven people, a team of horses and a wagon belonging to Daniel Haight on board. Of those passengers, one had been Reuben Haight, age sixteen, the son of Daniel Haight and Daniel's wife, Mary Dorland, and another had been their daughter. As the scow had been sinking, Reuben had immediately sprung into action. Mr. Wessel in a nearby skiff had seen what was happening and had come to their aid. Rueben had been able to swim with the victims one at a time to the awaiting skiff and in this way he had saved his family and another young girl. Despite his efforts, four of the passengers had drowned. The horses swam to shore but the wagon was lost.

Just three years later, on August 29, 1819, a big revival was scheduled at the Adolphustown Methodist Church. People came from all around the county to attend. Eighteen young people boarded a boat across from the church on Hay Bay. The bay was calm and clear that morning. About two hundred and seventy meters from the shore, the boat began to leak and filled quickly with water. As parents, friends, and neighbours watched helplessly on the shore, ten of the eighteen drowned that dreadful day. Only the eight who clung to the boat were eventually saved.

In 1938, Roy Jones was crossing the ice from Thessalon to Cockburn Island along with his passengers Mr. and Mrs. George Pateman, their baby, Edith, and three-year-old son, Lyle. The car plunged through the ice. Roy was able to jump clear, taking little Lyle with him. He tossed young Lyle onto the ice and made his way to Mrs. Pateman who was in the water. She was clinging to the ice with one hand and holding baby Edith with the other. Roy was able to pull Mrs. Pateman and Edith out. He then threw a blanket to Mr. Pateman and pulled him to safety. Roy's quick thinking surely saved them all.

In 1953, Walter Haight was making his way with his team across the ice to Richards Landing. The horses lost their footing and went down; they were unable to get back up. Walter made every effort to get the team up without success. Another team was summoned and hitched to the downed team. With great effort they were able to pull the team back up onto their feet.

Hay Bay Horse Ferry ca.1908.

Ferrying through the Years

Ferry service and steam ships to these isolated islands were their lifelines. Early ferries were not what we have today, but were canoes, skiffs, and scows. Taking passengers and small amounts of freight back and forth between the islands and the mainland was extremely important.

One interesting form of ferry was the horse-boat or team boat that ran at the narrow part of Hay Bay in Adolphustown. The service began around 1880 and carried on for about fifty years. This would have been a convenient way for Zachariah Haight and his son, Thomas, to bring their wheat to the

MV Glenora, formerly the St. Joseph Islander.

nearby mill. The same horse was used for twenty-seven of those years. The ferry could accommodate a team of horses and a wagon for fifty cents, and a single horse and buggy for twenty-five cents. The trip took five minutes. The paddles that were used to propel the boat were set in motion by two horses who trod on a circular table set flush with the deck at its centre. As the table revolved, it worked rollers which were connected to a shaft. This set the paddles in motion, which then propelled the vessel forward. The horses were stationary; the table on which they trod was furnished with ridges of wood that radiated like spokes from the centre. The horses caught these ridges of wood with their hooves as they walked in place, and this set the table in motion.

In the early 1800s, Captain Thomas Dorland, a distinguished United Empire Loyalist who was the brother of the father-in-law of Daniel Haight, petitioned to operate a ferry from his land in Adolphustown to the mills located on the opposite shore in Glenora. On April 27, 1802, permission was granted. Captain Dorland was ordered to furnish proper and complete crafts for ferrying passengers, cattle, carriages, and wares. Captain Dorland's ferry service operated from 1802 to 1825.

Of the many ferries used in the Bay of Quinte over the years, only the MV Glenora remains in operation today. Interestingly, in 1972 when a bridge was finally completed between St. Joseph Island and the mainland, the St. Joseph Islander was moved to Prince Edward County and became the MV Glenora. I've taken the Glenora ferry a few times and had strong feelings of nostalgia knowing that I had taken that same ferry to St. Joseph Island as a child to visit my grandparents Walter and Sarah Haight.

Steamboat ferry service was launched in 1879 to Cockburn Island and that would have been how Thomas Haight and Alzina Orser and their children arrived on Cockburn Island in 1885. A long list of passenger and freight vessels serviced the Island and the North Channel until the 1960s. The last of these vessels was the MS Norgoma which made trips from Owen Sound to Sault Ste. Marie with stops at Killarney, Little Current, Gore Bay, Meldrum Bay, Cockburn Island, Thessalon, Hilton Beach, and Richards Landing. Nowadays, visitors come to Cockburn Island by private boat and arrive at the municipal marina. They can also come by plane as the Island has a municipal grass airstrip. In the winter, when the water is frozen, snowmobiles are an option.

Ferry service to St. Joseph Island was first established in 1919. In 1933, another ferry called the Magic Carpet linked St. Joseph Island to Pine Island. In 1934, the government took over both ferries and made free ferry service available.

Walter Haight was a weekly vendor at the farmers market in Sault Ste. Marie. Before sunrise on Saturday morning, he would load up garden produce (in particular apples and corn when in season), catch the ferry, and drive the nearly seventy kilometers to the market. In the spring, there would occasionally be a two to three week delay in getting his maple syrup to market due to the lack of a ferry because of ice conditions. In 1952, a brand-new diesel ferry started providing year-round service. The Islander operated for twenty years.

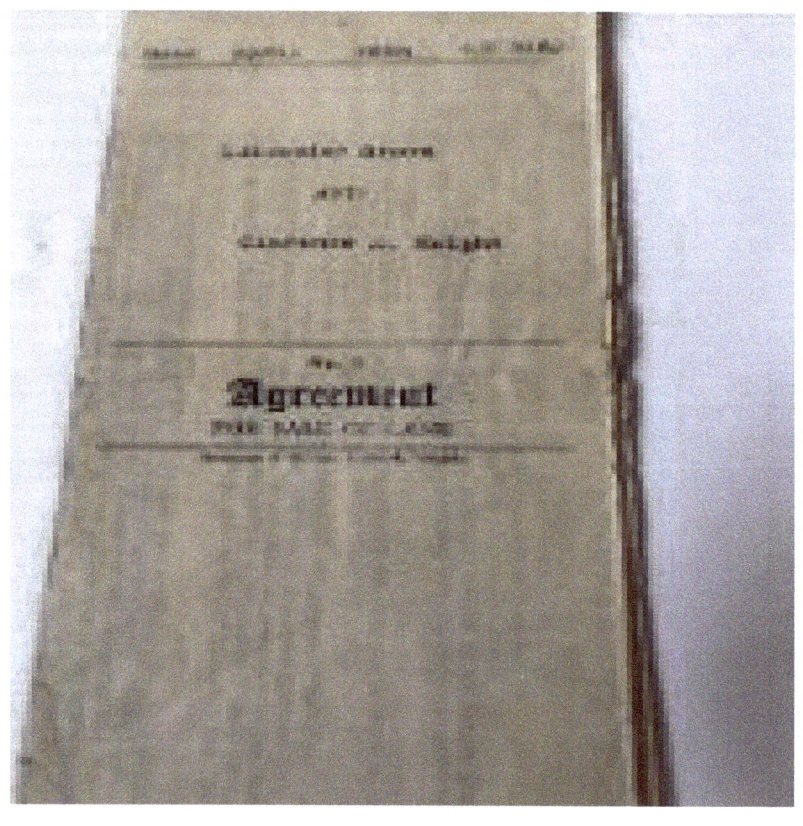

Sale agreement for Lot 11, Concession M between Alexander
Brown and Clarence Adelbert Haight, April 1930.

The House on Poverty Hill

The House on Poverty Hill, or the house on the mountain as it is sometimes referred to, is significant to my family history. Twenty different members of my maternal and paternal ancestors lived in this house from 1900 to 1957. It has had other owners since and remains a historic fixture today that holds fond memories for many of us of days gone by.

In 1930, Clarence Adelbert Haight and his wife, Jessie, bought a farm in Northern Ontario that brought the Haight descendants to St. Joseph Island. The story of this home takes many twists and turns. It all starts with the 1868 Free Grants and Homestead Act.

Ink drawing of Haight Homestead on Poverty Hill. H. Phillips, 1975

The Old Haight Homestead

H. Phillips / 75

The Act was established by the Province of Ontario to encourage settlers in Southern Ontario to move to Northern Ontario. It stated that every head of the family could obtain, on condition of settlement, a free grant of two hundred acres for himself and one hundred acres for each member of his family over the age of eighteen. Within the first five years, the settlers were required to clear and cultivate fifteen acres and to build a dwelling of at least sixteen feet by twenty feet in order to be granted title to the land.

The opportunity to own land had been a dream for my maternal two times great grandfather, John Brown, for many years. So, in 1878, after the death of his wife, Janet, he, along with his sons, John and Alexander, and two of his daughters, Mary and Sarah, headed to St. Joseph Island in Northern Ontario.

In 1883, John applied for a land patent, and in April of that year he was granted two hundred acres by the Crown (Lot 8 and Lot 9, Concession M). His son, John, applied and was granted Lot 10, Concession M. That same year, his son, Alexander "Sandy" Brown, purchased one hundred acres (Lot 11, Concession M) from Charles McArthur for $500. Many years later, to create work during the depression, men were hired for one dollar per day to flatten—by hand (for lack of equipment)—the hill on the steep roadway (10th Side Road) that goes by the property. Hence, this section of road became known as Poverty Hill.

It may be because the land had been purchased and had not been awarded through a land grant that Alexander (Sandy) was not required to follow the settlement rules, as it would be seventeen years before construction of the home began. Alexander (Sandy) Brown built a two-story house on Lot 11, Concession M in about 1900.

In 1929, due to his failing health and the untimely death of his youngest son, Launce, he put the farm up for sale and in 1930,

Del Haight, the son of Thomas Henry Haight, purchased it. The sale price was $1,500 with a payment of one hundred dollars upon the signing of the agreement. The balance of $1,400 was to be paid in annual instalments of one hundred dollars, plus interest, over the next fourteen years.

In 1935, Walter Haight and his wife Sarah took over the farm from Del and Jessie. For the next twenty-two years they worked hard and raised four children in the home. Donna Haight Hadden, the daughter of Walter and Sarah Haight, grew up in the house, and lived there from 1936 until the early 1950s. She recalls that there were two exterior doors, both of which faced the 10th Side Road and both of which led into the lower basement portion of the house. If you entered through one door, you found yourself in a smaller room where, when the family of Walter Haight lived there, the cream separator was kept.

Entering the second door took one into a much larger room with windows on both sides of the door. This was used as a living space for a short period. Beyond that room was a root cellar. There were wooden bunks filled with sand where potatoes, carrots, and other root vegetables were stored. The house was originally stucco, but in the 1970s, the owner, a Mr. Phillips, clad the house in board and batten which is well suited to the style of the house.

Over the years, the house has seen many changes. There have been additions, interior updates, and an adjustment to the exterior elevation. As well, the basement has been finished into a living and utility space. The current owner, Sheila Campbell, has lived in this wonderful old home since 1990, and has completed many updates to it.

The property has been divided like a peach pie over the years, with various members of both the Brown and Haight families, among others, owning parts of it. Currently, only fourteen and a half acres and the house remain from the original one hundred acres of Lot 11.

There are stories of the disagreements that occurred between the Haights and the Browns over the time that they lived as neighbours on these properties, though the situation was never as notorious as that of the Hatfields and McCoys. As the story was told to me, one disagreement involved the accessibility of water for cattle. I'm not certain whether it was a Haight or a Brown that happened to have a source of water on their land. The other party allowed their cattle to water there. There were some words exchanged; the offended party insisted that the offending party remove their cattle from the water source and provide water for the cattle on their own land.

Many years later, in 1952, the marriage between my parents Wilfred (Bill) George Haight and Emily Elizabeth Brown joined the two families and, as the saying goes, everyone lived happily ever after.

The Haights' Story Continues

For you to be born today, you have had a total of 16,382 ancestors over the last five hundred years. For you to exist in this present moment, think of all the struggles, battles, difficulties, and how much sadness that they went through, but think also of their stories of love, expressions of hope for the future, and happiness!

In order for you to be born, you need:

2 parents

4 grandparents

8 great grandparents

16 second great grandparents

32 third great grandparents

64 fourth great grandparents

128 fifth great grandparents

256 sixth great grandparents

512 seventh great grandparents

1,024 eighth great grandparents

2,048 ninth great grandparents

4,096 tenth great grandparents

8,192 eleventh great grandparents

Families are like branches on a tree. We grow in different directions, yet our roots remain as one. The Haights are scattered throughout Ontario these days, but we all come back to the familiar places of our ancestors whenever we can. There are still several Haight families in Prince Edward County and some descendants of the Cockburn Island Haights return there regularly, which keeps this a tight-knit group. They hold fundraisers throughout the year to maintain the historic buildings and they continue to both create new memories and relish telling the stories of days gone by.

Donna Haight Hadden was the last Haight to live on St. Joseph Island. She left there in 2007 and moved to Sault Ste. Marie. Donna was the last surviving child of Walter and Sarah Haight. With her passing in May of 2022 at the age of eighty-six, that generation vanished forever. They have all returned to St. Joseph Island as their final resting place.

The next generation have fond memories of the times that they spent with their grandparents and cousins. Summer picnics, Christmases, birthdays, and anniversaries were occasions when we all gathered. In the pursuit of jobs and education, some members of the Haight family have settled in more distant towns and cities. They will make new memories and stories which will be talked about in the years to come. Social media has allowed us to keep in touch, but it hasn't been quite the same as seeing everyone in person.

The Puritan and Quaker faiths have long disappeared, but faith is still important and is the foundation on which the Haights live their lives. Our parents and grandparents instilled in us the values that they learned from the generations before them, and hopefully we have done the same for our children.

The Haights were and are brave, confident, kind, and giving. They are entrepreneurs and craftsmen, community minded, and generous with their time and talents. This is a true testament to their values and character over the last five hundred years.

APPENDIX A

Family Quilt

Our family is a patchwork quilt, a lifetime being sewn

Each piece is an original, with beauty of its own

The brightest patches may be new and get the most attention

But the pieces that are loved and worn help give our quilt dimension

Threads of humour, faith, and love will keep our quilt together

To last in love throughout the years and wrap us close forever

Author Unknown

Whether near or far, we are bonded to our family. My hope is that our children and grandchildren will one day reminisce about their lives and also reflect on the history of the Haight family. This will hopefully give our children and grandchildren not only a greater understanding of the challenges and failures that our ancestors faced, but also of the successes that they enjoyed. I hope that our descendants will appreciate our ancestors' desire to survive and that together we will carry on the stories for generations to come.

Generations

1
Thomas Hoyte
Born: Seavington St. Mary, Somersetshire - 1520
Died: After 1575

2
Michael Hoyte
Born West Hatch, Somersetshire - 1560
Died West Hatch, Somersetshire - About 1624

3
Simon Hoyt
Born West Hatch, Somersetshire - 1590
Died Fairfield, Connecticut - About 1657

4
Moses Hoyt I
Born Fairfield, Connecticut - About 1634
Died Eastchester, New York - About 1712

5
Moses Hoyt II
Born Fairfield, Connecticut - About 1662
Died Eastchester, New York - About 1711

6
Moses Hoyt III
Born Eastchester, New York - About 1696
Died Stanford, Dutchess, New York - About 1751

7
Joseph Haight
Born Nine Partners, Dutchess, New York - About 1724
Died Washington, Dutchess, New York - 1817

8
Joseph Haight
Born Nine Partners, Dutchess, New York - 1746
Died Nine Partners, Dutchess, New York - About 1816

9
Joel Haight
Born Nine Partners, Dutchess, New York - About 1770
Died Adolphustown, Upper Canada - About 1829

10
Zachariah Haight
Born Hallowell, Upper Canada - About 1812
Died Hastings, Ontario, Canada - About 1900

11
Thomas Henry Haight
Born Hallowell, Upper Canada - About 1849
Dicd Thessalon, Ontario, Canada - About 1925

12
Clarence Adelbert Haight
Born Grand Rapids, Michigan - 1884
Died Hilton Beach, Ontario - 1954

13
Walter Stanley Haight
Born Cockburn Island, Ontario - 1908
Died Hilton Beach, Ontario - 1981

Family Members Elected or Appointed to Public Office

Michael Hoyte
Juryman (1606-1620), Tax Collector, Reeve

Moses Hoyte I
Land Surveyor (1670), Deputy Constable (1685), Town Commissioner (1686)

Daniel Haight
Clerk (1800)

Joel Haight
Pound Keeper (1800)

Thomas Haight
Councillor (1896),

Marshall Haight,
Councillor (1915)

Walter Haight
Pound Keeper (1946), Road Superintendent (1954)

Randall Haight
Councillor (1947)

David Haight
Councillor (1980), Reeve (2000)

www.ingramcontent.com/pod-product-compliance
Lightning Source LLC
Chambersburg PA
CBHW051631120626
46551CB00014B/2034